Ethical Investing

MODERNE
KULTUREN
RELATIONEN

Herausgegeben von Gerhard Droesser und Ruth Hutzel

BAND 22

PETER LANG

Manfred Stüttgen

Ethical Investing

Opportunities and Challenges of Morally Justified Investments

PETER LANG

Bibliografische Information der Deutschen Nationalbibliothek
Die Deutsche Nationalbibliothek verzeichnet diese Publikation in der Deutschen Nationalbibliografie; detaillierte bibliografische Daten sind im Internet über http://dnb.d-nb.de abrufbar.

Library of Congress Cataloging-in-Publication Data
A CIP catalog record for this book has been applied for at the Library of Congress.

ISSN 1619-358X
978-3-631-78905-6 (Print)
978-3-631-78961-2 (E-PDF)
978-3-631-78962-9 (EPUB)
978-3-631-78963-6 (MOBI)
DOI 10.3726/ b15969

Peter Lang – Berlin · Bern · Bruxelles ·
New York · Oxford · Warszawa · Wien

Diese Publikation wurde begutachtet.

www.peterlang.com

Preface

Ethical investing has been growing at an above-average rate for years. Two types of investors are contributing to the popularity of this specific investment style: The first type of investor has only financial objectives and may consider "ethical investing" merely one among many ways to reduce financial risk. He or she expects a better risk-adjusted return from sustainable investments. The second type of investor pursues financial objectives in the first place and social-ecological aspects as secondary objectives. In addition to financial performance, the investor seeks to have a positive impact on society and the environment. In practice, both motives here are closely intertwined. This study takes a closer look at the second motive.

If investors include moral norms and values as selection criteria in their investment decisions, how should they select and weigh up these norms and values? This question can only be answered meaningfully from the perspective of a moral philosophical theory. In practice, an answer can only be implemented wisely if an investor takes an independent stance in conflicts of investment standards. Alternatively, he or she can delegate responsibility to others, for example, to financial service providers or the supervisory authorities.

The present study advocates a step-by-step approach to the challenging topic of ethical investing, supported by the reader's own reason and judgement. Arguments that commit themselves solely to the primacy of financial goals, the primacy of legality or the primacy of laissez-faire are dismissed as being unconvincing. Instead, we recommend – as in other areas of life – a morally reflected practice in the area of investment. In line with Warren Buffett's instruction for a successful investor: Think for yourself!

A first edition (2014) and a second, revised edition (2017) of this book have been published in German. The analysis refers to the literature and experience with ethical investing in the German-speaking countries. However, the issues at hand could be equally relevant and helpful for the English-speaking reader.

The present translation has been inspired and supported by Georges Enderle and Joseph Holt, University of Notre Dame, Indiana/USA, and my colleagues Nicola Illi and Andreas Dietrich, Lucerne University of Applied Sciences and Arts, Institute of Financial Services Zug IFZ, Switzerland. I'd like to thank them for their active contribution in making this book accessible to a wider audience.

Manfred Stüttgen
Zug/Switzerland, June 4th, 2019

Contents

1 Ethical investing. What does it mean?

Ethical investing is a current trend. Almost every bank and fund provider offers investors a broad spectrum of investment forms that bear the label "ethics" in their product names. What exactly the unprotected term means is often opaque.

Upon closer inspection, however, the critical investor quickly realises that very different matters are subsumed under the umbrella term "ethics". Usually the investor is promised an investment process that integrates moral criteria. The result of this integration is then presented as an "ethical investment product". This product typically pledges a contribution to the investor's good conscience, in addition to an attractive return. There is often talk of clean returns, profits with a meaning, money improvement, double dividends, sustainable investment and good money, green money or sustainable money.

Is "ethical investing" a passing trend, or even a marketing strategy aimed at refurbishing the image of the financial services industry? Or, is it a responsible and effective investment of money, with the aim to direct capital in such a way that those involved promote moral goods and reduce morally objectionable behaviour?

The present study takes this type of reflection as an opportunity to analyse the following key questions.

- What moral principles can and *should* an investor base his investment behaviour on?
- What are the opportunities and what are the challenges of the justification and implementation of moral norms in investments?

The answers to these questions are intended to define starting points for a theoretical foundation and practical implementation of ethical investing, whereby moving at the scientific frontier of ethics in finance. The starting point as well as the goal of the present investigation lies in the practice of investing. The study seeks to provide orientation regarding the applied ethical question as to how an investor *should* behave in a concrete investment situation.

The following example illustrates the practical relevance as well as the difficulties that this study deals with.

Case study: With invested capital of 23 billion euros, the Versicherungsverein des Bankgewerbes (BVV) is the largest pension fund in Germany. In June 2013, BVV informed the approximately 135,000 insured individuals and pensioners about its investment policy.

> "BVV has always taken into account ethical, social, and ecological concerns in the investment process due to its long-term perspective and its obligations towards its members. However, they fall short of the regulatory objectives of return on investment, security and liquidity, which are required as a part of our mandate."[1]

The above quotation is intended to illustrate two different ideas as an introduction to the present study. First, in practice, the investment style of a large institutional investor appears to have a moral dimension. In this specific case, the investor even feels obliged to take a quasi-public stance on this dimension. Second, the example illustrates that the obligation to meet the ethical concerns, which are not further explained in this specific case, only has a limited binding effect compared to conventional investment criteria. Both observations are relevant in the context of the present study because they illustrate vividly – even if only anecdotally – possible opportunities and challenges of ethical investing.

The aims of this study are to illustrate the opportunities and challenges of so-called ethical investing systematically, to make them accessible to scientific scrutiny and to analytically reflect on them.

Despite its high level of practical relevance, the subject of this study has rarely been explored systematically. In addition to a dozen popular science guides on ethical investment, there are only a few scientific studies that comprehensively cover the topic. The present study would like to contribute to closing this gap.

1.1 Normative issues of investment. A scientific borderland

For many people, investing money is a worldly act of high practical significance, however, it is often met with little interest. The question of whether financial investments are affected by moral principles and if so, which ones,

1 BVV (2013), translated by the author [MS].

is rarely examined systematically from the point of view of economics and ethics.

Capital market theory as a special field of economics often presents itself as a value-free discipline. It rarely – if ever – reflects on its model assumptions and recommendations from an ethical perspective. Behavioural finance theory has recently integrated findings on the behaviour of investors into its models and thus distances itself from the unrealistic human image of Homo Economicus, which rationally maximises self-interest. Nevertheless, it does not succeed in adequately incorporating ethical questions into its models and discourses.[2]

Business ethics as a subfield of applied ethics reflects on the conditions and possibilities of moral economic action in a reason-based and normative way.[3] As a form of applied ethics, it seeks guidance in solving and evaluating practical moral problems. It also wants to increase the ability of ethical reflection in more complex contexts.[4]

However, the normative foundations of investor behaviour are a peripheral area of ethics in finance where research is rare. The topic is often dealt with in a non-academic way, in the form of popular scientific advice literature for the investor, providing practical stock market tips, specific product recommendations, contact persons and addresses and, in the better cases, background information on the morally justified purpose of the recommended investment.

In its long history, *moral theology* usually emphasises the instrumental value of money and warns against worshiping money as an end in itself. It recommends that the wealthy generously practice giving alms to the poor and needy. It also recognises avarice and greed in dealing with money as vices that promote egoism and harm humanity.[5] Since the medieval discourses on the morality of a creditor's interest claims,[6] however, the form

---

2 Cf. Schäfer (2011) 366 f. For behavioural aspects of investments in the context of ethical investing, cf. Scholand (2004) 139 ff. for further information.
3 Cf. Kersting (1994) 350; Dierksmeier (2006) 174; Pieper (2007) 98 f.
4 Cf. Assländer/Schumann (2011) 177 f.
5 Cf. Reinhardt (2009) 15, 31 and 38 ff.
6 Cf. Lücker (1999).

of financial investment has hardly been systematically investigated, except, at most, for the question of the morality of stock market speculation.[7]

While normative questions of financial investment are rarely analysed in academia, in financial practice there is a clear trend towards investments that bear the label of "ethics" in their name. The phenomenon of ethical investment is also attracting the attention of the media.

Today, ethical investing has a high level of practical relevance, which is countered by a theoretical deficit. The aim of this study is to make a contribution to closing this gap. The study intends to provide assistance and orientation for the practical question of how an investor should behave in a concrete situation.

In the absence of relevant moral principles for financial investments, however, this study cannot simply analyse and reflect on existing standards in their context of application. Rather, it must – methodically similar to theoretical ethical guidelines – also search for the justification of these principles and identify and reflect on bridging elements to mediate between theory and practice.

Before this concern is addressed, the terms ethics and morality will first be clarified in the following, since they are often used as interchangeable terms in everyday language. In some areas of society, especially in the economy, the term "ethics" is often preferred to the term "morality", because "ethics" seems to sound less strict and less morally narrow-minded. "Corporate ethics" and "ethical investment funds" are mentioned, unlike "corporate morality" or "moral funds".[8]

In contrast to this usage of language, it is customary to conceptually distinguish between ethics and morality in science. Ethics is understood here as a philosophical theory of morality, i.e., as a theory of reflection that refers to morality. Morality, on the other hand, is understood as a complex and multi-layered system of rules, norms and values that constitute the object of ethics. Accordingly, ethics stands on a meta-level to morality by analysing and reflecting on morality, postulating or criticising certain moral norms, and thus directly or indirectly intervening in the development of

7 As seminal study see von Nell-Breuning (1928) 127 ff.
8 Cf. Birnbacher (2013) 1.

morality from a superordinate point of view. Ethics sets itself in a position of distanced reflection both towards the socially accepted reality and to the principles advocated by individual moral philosophers.[9]

The object of ethics is thus moral (custom or convention) and morality (ethical order). Ethics does not refer to single actions or to what needs to be done in a particular case, but searches for moral principles and criteria for judging actions that claim morality and for the conditions under which moral norms and values are binding.[10] The object of morality, on the other hand, is the question of how people *should* act. Morality encompasses the totality of moral norms and values, customs and ideals, institutions and convictions with a claim to categorical validity and universal binding force.[11] The application of moral rules should contribute to the well-being of people and protect those affected by the actions of others.[12]

1.2 Financial and social-ecological dimensions are interconnected

The term ethical investment is initially understood as an umbrella term for investments that take selected moral criteria into account on top of financial investment criteria (risk, return, and liquidity). These criteria are usually of a social, ecological or cultural nature and aim to use the funds invested in strict compliance with the moral norms and values explicitly defined in each individual case.[13] Ethical investing aims to change conditions that are considered unfair, inhumane, environmentally destructive or unsustainable.[14]

The preceding definition emphasises the element of investing based on principles.[15] Since only an individual can reasonably reflect upon the selection and application of investment principles, it makes sense to primarily refer the term to the actions of an individual and not to an investment product itself. For this reason, this study mainly deals with the ethical

9 Cf. Birnbacher (2013) 2–4.
10 Cf. Pieper (2007) 28.
11 Cf. Horster (2012) 12; Birnbacher (2013) 7 ff; Thurnherr (2001) 67.
12 Cf. Horster (2009) 8 f.
13 Cf. Schäfer (2001b) 96; Pinner (2003) 19 and 28.
14 Cf. Gabriel (2012) 14.
15 Cf. Ulrich/Jäger/Waxenberger (1998) 8 f.

investment behaviour of a person. Thus, the actions and the corresponding responsibility of an investor are to be emphasised.

The term "ethical investment" or "ethical investing" seems to prevail in the current language despite its broad semantic field, which varies according to country, author, subject, and purpose of the use of the term. Frequent synonyms are responsible investing, investment adherent to principles, triple bottom line investing (referring to a threefold return to economic, ecological and social issues), social-ecological investment, socially responsible investment (SRI), social investment, sustainable investment, best-of-class investing, ESG (environmental, social and governance) investing[16] or, more recently, impact investing.[17] Some of these synonyms can be further differentiated so that, for example, in the special case of an ethical-ecological investment, so-called "green money" is now classified according to the varying shades light green and dark green in order to signal the efficiency in the implementation of selected criteria.[18]

Schäfer emphasises two aspects of the justice dimension of ethical investing. Intragenerational justice – especially between affluent industrialised and poor developing countries – and intergenerational justice between the present and future generations.[19]

In an empirical study, Gabriel points out that important players in the financial market, for example the providers of sustainability indices, often differentiate the preceding terms according to the addressees rather than the objects. He elaborates on this as follows.

> "The differentiation of these terms ... is made in such a way that the use of the term 'ethical investment' is rather attributed to actors from the religious environment, the use of the term 'socially responsible investment' is rather attributed to actors from the social sphere and the use of the term 'sustainable investment' is rather attributed to actors from the environmental sphere."[20]

Ott stresses that, strictly speaking, one cannot speak of an ethical investment, but at best a moral or morally justified investment. In the absence of

16 Cf. Pinner (2003) 20–23; Scholand (2004) 66 f.
17 Cf. Schäfer (2012) 24; Oehri (2012) 1; Forstinger (2013) 28.
18 Cf. Scholand (2004) 122.
19 Cf. Schäfer (2001a) 740 f.
20 Gabriel (2005) 14, translated by the author [MS], cf. also Gabriel (2007) 161.

alternatives, he nevertheless recommends adopting the term ethical investment – even if it is viewed critically – for practical reasons.[21] This consideration is followed by the present study, so that the term ethical investing or investment is to be used in the broad sense defined above.

1.3 Historical development and first approaches to moral justification

1.3.1 Faith-based investing for humanity and fair distribution

The roots of ethical investment can historically be traced back to religious communities investing money in accordance with religious norms and values. LOUCHE ET AL. therefore describe the religious communities as the pioneers of ethical investing, who have been practicing this in the form of faith consistent investing for centuries. LOUCHE ET AL. roughly distinguish the following three religious movements and precursors of ethical investments.[22]

(1) The *Jewish and Catholic traditions*, which began 3,500 years ago to demand justice, equality, and fairness as criteria for lending money.[23]
(2) *Islamic banking and Sharia-compliant investing*, which has developed since the 7th century CE and according to which financial transactions must be compliant with Islamic norms and values. This excludes, for example, investments in producers of pork products, weapons and alcohol, pornography and parts of the entertainment industry for being inadmissible, as well as the collection of interest, which is considered usury.[24]
(3) The *tradition of the Christian free churches*, especially the Quakers and Methodists, who since the middle of the 18th century have emphasised that to handle money responsibly is already considered an extremely high priority in the New Testament. In 1758 the Quakers forbade their members to participate in the slave trade.[25] In 1760, in his paper titled

21 Cf. Ott (1997) 224.
22 Cf. Louche et al. (2012) 301 f.
23 Cf. Louche et al. (2012) 301.
24 Cf. Duchrov (2010) 90–93; Maniera (2013) 31.
25 Cf. Cunningham (2001) 71.

"The use of money" and with reference to LUKE 16, 9, the founder of the Methodists, JOHN WESLEY, recommended to observe ethical standards when investing money. He urged the parishioners to make profits...

„... not at the expense of life nor at the expense of our health nor with hurting our mind. Therefore we may not engage or continue in any sinful trade; any that is contrary to the law of God, or of our country ... hurting our neighbour in his substance, nor by hurting our neighbour in his body ... nor by hurting our neighbour in his soul."[26]

To this day, the Methodists preserve principles such as the observance of human rights, fair trade, environmental protection, and medical safety in their investments. In 1971, they launched their first major investment fund, the PAX WORLD FUND, which excludes investments in weapons, alcohol and gambling and is regarded as a precursor to professional ethical investing and the establishment of so-called negative investment criteria also known as exclusion criteria.[27]

1.3.2 Politically motivated investments against apartheid and Vietnam War

In the 1970s, ethically motivated investment was also practiced in the USA by the anti-apartheid and anti-Vietnam War movements. In this case, political goals were formulated as exclusion criteria to help avoid investments in unjust regimes in South Africa or to weaken arms suppliers to warfare in Vietnam. The success in exerting economic pressure on the apartheid regime led a number of ethical US funds to include negative selection criteria, for example with regard to the discrimination against women or minorities, animal experiments or nuclear power.[28]

1.3.3 Social and ecological investments for human beings and the environment

In Europe, ethical investments developed out of the environmental, peace, and civil rights movements in the 1980s. Many activists not only want to

---

26 Quoted from Sparkes (2001) 84.
27 Cf. Sparkes (2001) 84 f; Louche et al. (2012) 301 f.
28 Cf. Schneeweiss (1998) 89 f.

demonstrate against rearmament, environmental degradation and racial discrimination, but also want to support their ethically motivated claims by (re-)allocating their money. Funds are to be invested for projects that appear ecologically and socially sustainable. At first, these included environmentally friendly, sustainable technologies,[29] and later, for instance, microfinance investments that fight poverty in developing countries.[30] The formulation of positive criteria gains influence, i.e., not only those investments that appear to be morally unfavourable are excluded from the investment universe (negative selection) but those investments which are regarded as particularly valuable for moral reasons are specifically included in this case (positive selection).[31]

In the Anglo-Saxon countries, ethical investing now has a market share of more than ten percent of total assets. In the German-speaking countries, the market share is still significantly smaller, lying in the lower single digit percentage range, though showing very high growth.[32] In line with the increasing size and high growth rates in the field of ethical investments, an increasing differentiation of the players and their motives can be observed.[33]

---

29 Cf. Deml/Blisse (2011) 1; Rotthaus (2009) 40–42 on the timeline of ethical-ecological investments.
30 Cf. Missbach (2007) 101 ff; cf. Stüttgen (2019a) 117.
31 Cf. Schneeweiss (1998) 90.
32 Cf. n.s. (2013a) 28; Arbeitsgruppe DBK (2010) 10 f; Scherhorn (2008) 45.
33 Cf. Stüttgen/Mattmann (2017) 77–87; Stüttgen/Mattmann (2018) 8–18.

2 Factual challenges for ethical investing

Chapter 1 introduced the subject of analysis and presented its historical roots. Chapter 2 analyses the opportunities and challenges of ethical investing from a factual and practical perspective. Chapter 3 continues with a theoretical reflection on the moral criteria of investment activities and the normative status of ethical investing from a moral-philosophical point of view.

2.1 Investors want to influence the conduct of investment targets

The aim of this study is to reflect ethically on investment activities. For this purpose, it is first assumed that an investor potentially bears a moral responsibility for the use of the funds made available by him, an assumption that we will have to examine more closely.

In order to be able to coherently argue for such a shared responsibility, in a first step a simplified causal chain of the complex interdependencies in ethical investing should be reconstructed. Modelling such a causal chain involves selection decisions, the most important of which are listed below.

At the centre of the chain of actions lie the private investors, financial institutions, and companies trading on capital markets, along with their actions and their moral justification. An investment process, however, is structured in several stages. For example, an investor can invest money with a bank or – directly or indirectly – in a mutual fund. The manager of a mutual fund can use this money to invest in companies – in the form of equity or debt capital. Depending on the type of investment, the corresponding companies as the objects of investment, can use the capital for their own purposes in different ways. Even this greatly simplified description shows that some decisions are necessary in order to narrow down the object of analysis.

In the following, the narrowing down of the object of analysis and thus also the modelling of the cause–effect relationship between the investor and the corresponding use of funds by the objects of investment can be guided by two ideas. First, fundamental connections between the micro level of

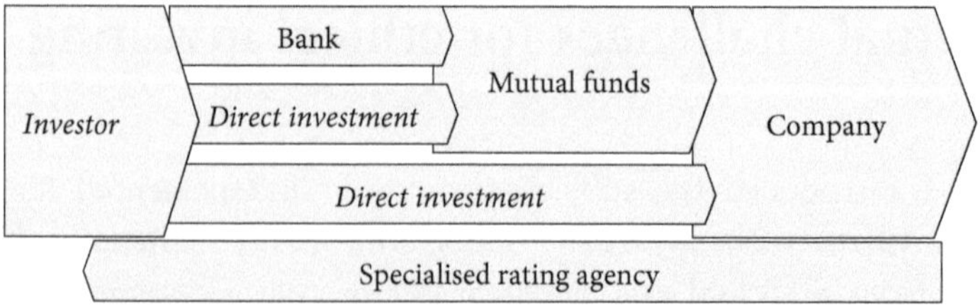

Figure 1: Interrelationships and actors in ethical investing.

the individual investor and the meso level of social collectives – companies and industries – are to be examined. Secondly, typical and generalizable cause-and-effect relationships of ethical investing will be investigated.

In this sense, a private investor and his investment activities are chosen as the point of reference for our analysis. Compared to an institutional investor a private investor is subject to fewer restrictions and thus to fewer potential conflicts of objectives. Narrowing down the analysis to the perspective of a private investor will help us cope with the complexity of the subject matter.

2.2 Interdependencies in ethical investing

The attribution of moral responsibility to the investor for the actions of the objects of investment assumes an appropriate causal relationship between the investment and the actions of the objects of investment. Figure 1 shows the key players in a highly simplified causal chain starting with the investment and ending in the use of funds. This model should serve to determine the existence of a causal relationship between the investment activity of an investor and the activity of companies as the objects of investment. The attribution of responsibility to an investor assumes an underlying causal responsibility.[34]

The investor should stay at the centre of the analysis, be it a private or an institutional investor (e.g., pension fund, foundation, church). Typically, the groups differ not only in the size of their assets (a relevant threshold

34 Cf. Birnbacher (1995) 90. For theories of causality cf. also Birnbacher/Hommen (2012) 39 ff.

can be set, for example, at 30–50 million US dollars in assets), but also in the objectives and motives of their investment. Institutional investors, for instance, often have to take into account the purpose tied to their funds, which is derived from the objectives of their institution.[35] Our considerations are based on the simpler case of the private investors, who only have to take their own goals into account when making investment decisions.

Private investors have a wide range of investment vehicles at their disposal, from simple to very complex financial products. Savings accounts or fixed-term deposits, investment funds, shares of listed companies, fixed income securities of companies or governments, structured investment products, direct investments in unlisted companies (private equity, venture capital), and hedge funds, to name just a few examples. The investor can choose between these investment forms and invest his disposable assets either indirectly via a bank or as a direct investment. For the purpose of this study, it is assumed that the investor invests in companies. In this case, the specific features of ethical investing can be illustrated particularly well. Investments in shares are made either as a direct equity stake in a company or indirectly via mutual funds investing in company equity.[36]

By investing in equity shares, the investor becomes a co-owner of a company. In a legal sense, the investment provides a company with equity capital that serves as risk capital and represents an important prerequisite for the company's economic activities. In return for providing capital, the shareholder receives the right to participate in profits (dividends). In addition, he benefits from various membership rights, e.g., the right to information about the development of the business and the right to vote at the general assembly.[37]

For our study it is assumed that an investor is linked to the management of a company by a causal relationship, due to the fact that he provides

35 Cf. Ulrich et al. (1998) 13–16 on the different motives of these types of investors.
36 The investor's direct involvement in shares is usually also handled by a bank or broker in listed stock corporations. However, for the purpose of the present study, further clarification is not required.
37 On the co-responsibility of shareholders, see Hoffmann/Scherhorn (2002) 13.

capital to a consciously selected company and thus makes a contribution to that company being able to pursue its activity.[38]

The theoretical question as to what degree of causality the provision of capital has for the specific (morally assessable) actions of companies can remain open at this point. In practice, the answer to this question will depend in particular on the absolute or relative size of a company's equity exposure. In many cases, the causal influence of a shareholding in a company may only be classified as a marginal condition in a larger causal complex, as the actions of a company are multifactorial in nature and individual causes are difficult to isolate. If, however, the provision of capital is considered to be merely a negligible secondary factor in the economic activities of companies, there is a risk of losing sight of the interdependency between an equity investment and its influence on the actions of a company.

Birnbacher points out that subjective factors and perspective always come into play when differentiating between causes and constraints.[39] In one case, providing capital to a company may be perceived as "the" cause, in another case as a secondary condition of economic activity. For the purpose of our investigation, however, the provision of capital should be understood as an important partial cause within the framework of ethical investing.

2.2.1 The freedom of the investor in choosing a bank and an investment

In the simplified model of a chain of actions from the investment decision made by the investor to the use of the funds by companies, the investor can ideally make three decisions. (1) The choice of the bank, (2) the choice of the mutual fund that invests in equities according to certain selection criteria or (3) the direct choice of the company shares in which the investor wishes to invest.

---

38 Whether a shareholder acquires a share at the time of the issue or after its issue, i.e. on the secondary market, is irrelevant for this argument, even if this distinction is occasionally made in the literature.

39 Cf. Birnbacher (1995) 83 f.

In order to select the desired investment, first the investor needs information about the potential objects of investment. On the one hand, these are financial key performance indicators. In the case of ethical investments, on the other hand, this is information on the use of the funds by the mutual fund or the respective company. Investors – as well as their bank, mutual funds or any other interested party – can obtain information on a company's ethical conduct through specialised rating agencies, e.g., ISS-OEKOM, INRATE or the SÜDWIND INSTITUTE to name just a few.[40] These specialised rating agencies assess the business conduct of companies, mutual funds or banks, based on their self-disclosure or publicly available information, and make these analyses and assessments available to investors in exchange for a fee.[41]

The precondition for the investor's freedom of choice is that there are genuine alternatives for action in his own situation. In most industrialised countries with developed capital markets, this requirement is well met. The number of investment alternatives typically increases with the size of the assets available. This applies in particular to the various possibilities of direct participation in companies in a form other than shares. Such a direct investment (private equity, venture capital) is usually only available for investments above a certain size.

2.2.2 Responsibility based on the social obligation inherent in ownership

The fundamental freedom of the investor in the choice of a banking relationship and investment opportunity does not directly imply the attribution of responsibility in a moral sense. A normative attribution of responsibility requires not only a subject of responsibility (e.g., investor, company) and an object (e.g., investment activity, production of goods), but also an instance of responsibility (e.g., fellow human beings, conscience) and a reference to certain normative standards (foundation of norms).[42]

---

40 Cf. Stüttgen/Mattmann (2018) 41–61 for a comprehensive overview of rating agencies.

41 Cf. Schneeweiss (2002) 101 f; Schneeweiss (1997) 342–345; Pinner (2003) 140 f; Gabriel (2007) 133–136.

42 Cf. Werner (2011c) 543; Ulshöfer (2008) 32.

In order to be able to outline a possible joint responsibility for morally judged actions of private investors or companies in the context of ethical investing, in a first step it is necessary to set out some important basic assumptions and cause–effect relationships.

In most industrialised nations, private property and economic freedom are protected by the law, for example in Switzerland, by Articles 26 and 27 of the Swiss Federal Constitution. In some countries, the legal protection of property goes hand in hand with obligations tied to private property. For example, Article 14(2) of the German Basic Law stipulates: "Property entails obligations. Its use shall also serve the public good." Such a social commitment, if stipulated at all, is often neither clearly defined, nor further specified or claimed by the corresponding law to the same extent as is the case for property rights of private individuals or corporations.[43]

The protected property rights and economic freedom of private individuals and corporations are therefore not matched by equally comprehensive rights to protect social capital (e.g., workers, children, local cultural assets) or natural capital (e.g., soil, water, animal species, ecosystems) in most countries in the West, and even less so in poor countries and regions in the South. As a consequence of this disparity between rights and obligations, companies often use their leeway within legal grey areas of entrepreneurial action in favour of the interests of private capital (e.g., to achieve higher returns in the interest of their shareholders) at the expense of the general public or nature. They produce negative externalities (e.g., financial crises, environmental degradation, health hazards to employees) without being held legally accountable by a court of law. In this case, production costs are passed on to the environment or society and profits are monopolised. The primary financial beneficiaries of this redistribution are the owners of financial capital, e.g., the shareholders of companies.[44]

---

43 Cf. Scherhorn (2009a) 239–241; Scherhorn (2009b) 22–26. Scherhorn points out that although the German Basic Law recognises the social link between property and society, private law only shows selective correspondences (e.g., tenancy law, occupational health and safety), so that in Germany too, capital takes precedence over other production factors.

44 Cf. Scherhorn (2008) 42 f; Scherhorn (2009a) 242 f; Scherhorn (2009b) 23; Scherhorn (2010) 5 f.

In other words, the global legal framework allows companies to enrich themselves with common goods and violate people's social rights or cause lasting damage to the natural environment in select countries. Well-established moral criteria such as human rights or the preservation of the environment can be violated without those responsible being sanctioned.[45]

There are numerous examples of this phenomenon. They range from the violations of human rights in open-cast copper and gold mining in the Philippines by the globally active Swiss-British commodity group GLENCORE,[46] to harmful labour practices by the Californian company APPLE at its production sites in China, to major environmental catastrophes such as the nuclear accident in Fukushima by the co-responsible operator TEPCO, or the destruction of entire ecosystems by oil spills of unknown magnitude by companies such as ROYAL-DUTCH/SHELL or BP.

In essence, these cases deal with problems of distributive justice and the fairness of institutions. The costs and benefits of the production factors capital, labour, and ecological environment are unfairly distributed in the sense that capital is privileged unilaterally over the other two factors. The institutions of law and the market unfairly grant private property rights at the expense of social and environmental factors. The root of the problem therefore lies in policy failure or market failure.

Against this background, however, our discussion about ethically responsible investment does not begin at the macro level. It does not seek to directly influence changes in legal and political frameworks and to address the rules and practices of unjust social institutions on a macro level. The discussion about the responsibility of an investor in the context of ethical investment focuses rather on the meso level of the actions of companies and industries, as well as the micro level of the individual decisions of the single investor. Ethical investment does not seek to functionally replace a necessary reform of the political-legal regulation of economic activities from above, but rather to accentuate and complement it from below.[47]

---

45 Cf. Scherhorn (2008) 40.
46 Cf. n.s. (2013b) 13.
47 Cf. Ott (1997) 210 f. In this sense, Berg (2011) 326 f defines ethical investment as a political process too. On different dimensions of ethical investment at the individual, institutional, and economic levels cf. Stüttgen (2019b) 19–22.

In this context, the concept of responsibility encompasses a moral quality on top of its legal substance. However, nowadays the subject of action and the subject of responsibility are often split in an increasing number of different contexts.[48] This separation of the subject of action and the subject of responsibility is partially given in the investment of funds in a special case. Analytically, a distinction must be made here between the investment activity of an investor on the one hand and the responsibility of companies as corresponding objects of investment for morally assessable activity on the other.[49] Decisive for a possible attribution of moral co-responsibility to the investor is the answer to the question whether and – if so – how the investor can influence the morally assessable actions of companies by choosing his concrete investment.

2.2.3 Impact on capital costs and company image

The choice of investment can essentially have an impact on the moral conduct of companies and management in two ways. First, it can influence the cost of capital, i.e., the (re)financing costs of the company and thus indirectly its profitability. Secondly, it can shape the image of a company that adheres to or violates certain moral norms.[50] Both effects are plausible, although the quantitative relationship between selected variables might be difficult to validate empirically.

(1) Impact on the cost of capital

When ethically oriented investors buy shares from companies who comply with moral standards, these companies' share price tends to rise. The share price is – among many other things – a valid indicator of the costs of raising funds, i.e., the cost of capital. The higher the share price and the more valuable a company is, the easier it is to raise equity at attractive conditions, i.e., the lower its cost of capital. The lower the cost of capital, the higher the profitability of a company and the higher the potential payouts, e.g., management salaries or dividends to shareholders.[51]

---

48 Cf. Holderegger (1992) 204 and 202.
49 Cf. Schaefers (2013) 29 and 115.
50 Cf. Schneeweiss (2002) 114–117; Döpfner (2000) 196 f; Hoffmann (2004) 22.
51 Cf. Arbeitsgruppe DBK (2010) 18 f.

Ethical investing can use this interdependence to create certain incentives for the management of a company to assume its moral responsibility as comprehensively as possible. The strength of the incentive and the impact is functionally dependent on the size and number of ethically oriented investors who exercise their influence, on the liquidity and transparency of the capital market, and on the specific situation of the company.

(2) Impact on the image of a company

Ethical investment can have an impact not only on financing costs but also on the image of a company. The inclusion of a company in an ethics fund and a good performance in an ethically based rating can have a positive impact on a company's reputation with the public, with clients and in the financial market. Conversely, negative image effects can occur when ethically motivated investors put public pressure on a company because its business practices are morally doubtful. In the particular case of an ethically motivated boycott, not just the image but also the business of a company can be tarnished.[52]

(Large) shareholders, ethical investment funds or ethical rating and research agencies can also seek to communicate critical views directly with the management of a company and thus influence the business policy of a company. It is precisely this type of influence that appears to be effective in addressing weaknesses in companies and constructively implementing improvements in practice.[53]

2.2.4 Investment strategies to shape the moral conduct of companies

Ethical investing aims to shape the business practices of companies so that they are compliant with fundamental moral norms and values. The goal of ethical investing can therefore be described as influencing the use of capital and the actions of companies according to moral criteria.

For this purpose, when selecting a financial investment, the investor – or the bank or fund manager as the agent of the investor – can apply specific investment strategies. They may invest according to the principles of negative or positive selection, which have already been developed to some extent

52 Cf. Schneeweiss (2002) 114–117; Arbeitsgruppe DBK (2010) 19.
53 Cf. Schneeweiss (2002) 116 f; Arbeitsgruppe DBK (2010) 19.

Controversial business activities	*Controversial business practices*	*Controversial activities in a country*
• Weapons/armament • Abortion • Atomic energy • Biocides • Organochlorine bulk products • Embryo research • Gambling • Green genetic engineering • Production of addictive substances (tobacco etc.) • …	• Human rights abuse • Child labour • Violations of labour law • Environmentally harmful production processes • Animal testing • Corruption • Accounting fraud • Cartel infringement • …	• Death penalty • Authoritarian regimes • Atomic energy • No climate protection • Euthanasia • Severe money laundering • Serious corruption • Serious human rights violations • …

Figure 2: Exclusion criteria to guide negative selection. Based on Kohrs/Grün (2008) 134. See also Assländer/Schenkel (2009) 51 f.

in the historical precursors of ethical investing. Alternatively, the investor can use the "best-in-class" selection principle.

Negative selection, positive selection and best-in-class approach

(1) *Negative selection.* With this approach, the investor excludes (=filters) certain objects of investment from the investment universe according to moral criteria. These may be companies engaged in controversial business activities (e.g., nuclear energy), companies engaged in controversial business practices (e.g., violations of labour law), or entire countries engaged in controversial activities (e.g., serious human rights violations). Figure 2 gives an overview of possible exclusion criteria for ethical investing.[54]

(2) *Positive selection.* In this approach, the investor selects those objects of investment that he considers particularly worthy of promotion. This category can include, for example, companies that fight poverty and support development projects or that develop innovative products

54 Cf. Kohrs/Grün (2008) 133 f; Schneeweiss (2002) 90–95.

that meet specific moral concepts in a certain way (e.g., ecological sustainability).[55]

(3) *Best-in-class approach.* Here the investor allocates capital with those companies that act in a particularly exemplary way relative to peers in the same sector, e.g., measured by criteria of social compatibility or environmental protection.[56]

A well-informed investor can exercise the above-mentioned approaches either directly himself or indirectly by assigning a financial intermediary as his agent. The three approaches are not mutually exclusive, but can be combined and are often used in combination in practice.[57]

Negative selection, positive selection, and best-in-class investing are investment strategies to select companies according to morally justified criteria. Two special cases of positive company selection are "affinity banking" and "impact investing". In contrast to impact investing, affinity banking is not an investment, but the selection of the financial intermediary, in this case the bank.[58] As the agent of the investor, the bank plays an important role in the implementation of the investor's moral objectives. Both affinity banking and impact investing may be suitable for increasing the impact of investment strategies based on ethical motives. They have recently enjoyed increasing popularity in practice.

Affinity banking and impact investing as means to enhance effectiveness

In so-called affinity banking, the investor selects the bank that corresponds to or is close to his own moral norms and values in key points of corporate policy, management, and culture. Examples of such financial institutions are the ALTERNATIVE BANK SWITZERLAND, the UMWELTBANK in Germany, the ETHIKBANK operating in Germany and Austria, and the BANK FÜR ORDEN UND MISSION in Idstein, Germany.[59]

---

55 Cf. Schneeweiss (2002) 91 and 95 ff.

56 Cf. Kohrs/Grün (2008) 133 f.

57 For the influence of sustainable investors on companies, cf. Schneeweiss (2017) 133 f.

58 Cf. Schäfer (2011) 373 f on the concept of affinity as a selection criterion for banks.

59 Cf. Rotthaus (2009) 88–96 and Weber (2017) 272–276 for an overview of the banks mentioned and their corresponding product range.

The ALTERNATIVE BANK SWITZERLAND, for example, explicitly prioritises ethical principles before profit maximisation. It has set itself the important goals of satisfying basic human needs and preserving the natural environment. To this end, it provides loans to finance ecological and social projects, which are granted at more favourable terms with the help of its investors' solidarity.[60]

Impact investing is a special form of the positive selection of investments. In this case, the socially or ecologically motivated investment should have a clearly measurable effect on the investor's ethically justified objective.

Impact investing often consists of a mixture of financially oriented investing and philanthropically oriented project financing. Impact investing is currently being established in North America as a popular form of ethical investing – an estimated 100+ billion US dollars are currently invested through impact investments – and has also spread into German-speaking countries. Impact investing can refer to various forms of investment and is increasingly being developed not only by institutional investors, in particular foundations, but also by private investors.[61]

SCHÄFER cites a participation in the Indian energy producer HUSK POWER SYSTEMS (HPS) as an example of an impact investment. HPS has a technology that generates electricity from rice husks. The investment promotes geographic expansion so that more than 1.25 million people in 1,000 Indian villages can be supplied with electricity from HPS's mini power plants. The electric light produced in this way is not only cheaper for the poor population, it is also emission-free, unlike the old kerosene lamps.[62]

Impact Investing also promotes other important issues in developing countries, such as access to clean drinking water, education, and improved medical care.[63]

OEHRI differentiates between two forms of impact that an impact investment can have. First, the investment has an effect on those who use the invested money (so-called push impact). Secondly, the investment has an

60 Cf. Rotthaus (2009) 91 f and Diaz (2017) 247 ff.
61 Cf. Schäfer (2012) 24; Oehri (2012) 1; Auerswald/Quadir (2011); Rockefeller Foundation (2012).
62 Cf. Schäfer (2012) 24.
63 Cf. Schäfer (2012) 24.

effect on the investor himself (pull impact). In the second case, dealing with this special form of ethical investment provides an impulse to fundamentally think about the criteria of investment, to reform them if necessary, and thus to create a consistency between the investor's self-image, his moral norms and values, and his investment policy.[64]

Given the interrelationships between investor and investment objects discussed so far: How can an investor assess whether the use of the funds in an investment is really in line with moral norms and values?

In practice, two fundamental issues arise here: First, a principal-agency problem, which mainly presents itself as a problem of the implementation of already defined criteria. Secondly, there is the problem of defining appropriate ethical investment criteria and monitoring their implementation. Both problems will be examined in more detail below.

2.2.5 Control issues and information asymmetries as key challenges

The above explanations have shown that financial intermediaries often act as agents for the investor. If the investor is not directly involved in a company, his funds are usually allocated through a bank or an ethical investment fund. But even when directly involved as an investor in a company, a company's management ultimately controls the use of the investor's funds. The investor's influence and control in comparison to the employees and management of a company remain limited. A company may procure inputs from other companies as its value chain is based on the division of labour. Or the company is a diversified conglomerate.[65] The company may also produce products that can be used for different purposes ("dual use"), some of which are morally controversial. It could, for instance, produce centrifuges that can be used for the enrichment of uranium, for both military and civilian use. In each of these cases, the challenges mentioned above multiply, further reducing the investor's influence and control.

This raises the practical problem of information asymmetry and a lack of control between the investor as a principal and his agents. Agents can be the bank or the manager of an ethical investment fund or the management

64 Cf. Oehri (2012) 1.
65 Cf. Gabriel (2008) 30 f.

of the company in which the investor invests. Since the contractual relationships between the parties involved are incompletely defined, the agents can exploit existing information asymmetries opportunistically and discretionarily in favour of their own interests and at the expense of the investor. Ethical investing is thus an example of the principal agent theory, which has emerged in the social sciences as an important model for explaining human action in institutions.[66]

Although the motives of the bank, the ethical investment fund or the company can also be of a moral nature, they do not have to be and in practice probably not always are. Each of the agents involved can pursue completely self-interested goals – e.g., of an economic nature – and for this reason alone falsely simulate morally correct behaviour to the investor or other stakeholders.

Even in the most favourable case where the agents' motives coincide with those of the investor, the asymmetric information situation between the parties involved does not sufficiently ensure that the investor's objectives are prioritised, weighted, and implemented "correctly". The investor suffers from a lack of control over the actions of the company in which he invests.

A principal-agent problem of this kind can be solved through the design of appropriate incentives, information systems, and control systems, though it cannot be mitigated completely.

In the case of ethical investments, a high level of transparency regarding the compliance with ethical criteria is an important confidence-building element to at least partially reduce existing information asymmetries. A contribution to the necessary level of transparency can be ensured through the company ratings of ethical rating agencies. In addition, elements of good corporate governance can increase the desired level of control, such as the creation of an independent advisory board of experts that regularly reviews the definition of and compliance with moral criteria for corporate management on the basis of appropriate structures and processes.[67] However, the more elements and agents there are in the chain of actions between the

66 Cf. Jensen/Meckling (1976) 305 ff; cf. also Schäfer (2011) 372 f in the context of ethical tensions in banks and Brodbeck (2006) 90–93 with reference to the topic of corporate governance.

67 Cf. Pinner (2003) 137–152 and 103 ff.

investment activity and the activity of a company as a corresponding object of investment, the more serious the principal-agent problem becomes for the investor.

The described approaches of affinity banking and impact investing are also suitable for mitigating the principal-agent problem and its consequences, at least partially. In affinity banking, the verifiable consistency between the moral principles, values, and norms of the investor and those of the bank can create a certain basis of trust that the bank is acting in the investor's interest. In impact investing, control over the use of funds is increased by shortening the chain of actions between the investment and use of funds wherever possible and by introducing specific key performance indicators to monitor the effect of the investment on the use of funds in a timely manner.

Irrespective of the control level that the investor can exercise, the question of the concrete objectives of an ethical investment arises. This is to be examined below.

2.3 Investment objectives and conflicting investment objectives

2.3.1 Return, risk, liquidity, and use of funds

The aim of a conventional investment is to optimise the three objectives of return (investment performance), risk and liquidity (availability). From a classical point of view, the optimal investment offers high return, high liquidity, and low risk. In practice, trade-offs exist between these objectives, i.e., one objective can only be achieved at the expense of another. For example, a higher return is only achieved if the investment risk is higher or if the liquidity of the investment is lower. The tension between the three goals is therefore also referred to as the magic triangle.[68]

In ethical investing, the three goals of conventional investing are extended by a fourth objective, namely the moral responsibility of the use of funds, which is expressed by the action of a company as an object of investment. One then speaks of the magic square, because there is also a trade-off between the moral responsibility of entrepreneurial action, which the

68 Cf. Pinner (2003) 28.

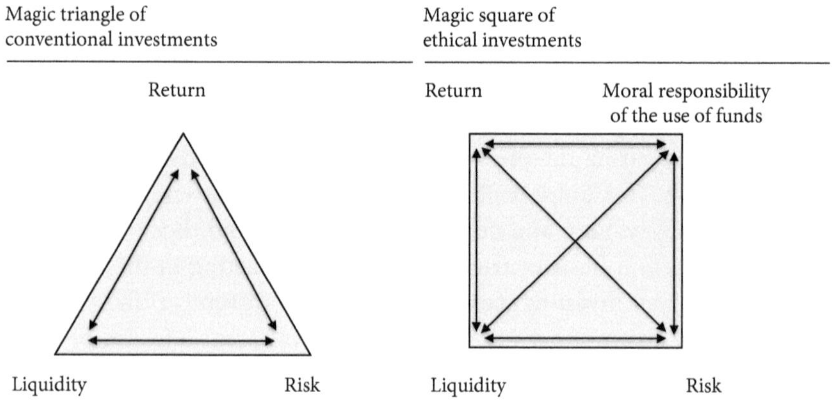

Figure 3: Conflicting objectives of financial investments. Based on Pinner (2003) 28 and Cengiz et al. (2010) 263.

investor tries to influence, and the other three variables in practice. In most cases, the tension between yield on the one hand and the morally compliant use of funds on the other is emphasised as potentially the most important conflict of objectives.[69]

Figure 3 illustrates the conflicts between the three targets of conventional investments and the four targets of ethical investments.

From the perspective of economics and ethics, handling the conflicts between financial and morally justified goals is not only investigated in the concrete application presented here. Even the more general case is controversial in the basic theoretical discussion. Derived from the basic discussion,[70] two extreme positions for an investor's actions can be distinguished with regard to our concrete application.

(1) The investor does not even consider the goal of the responsible use of funds or, if he does, considers it at best an equal (optimisation) goal to the financial goals, which may have to be integrated for instrumental reasons. In this case, the scope of morality is limited by the financial objective pursued.

69 Cf. Pinner (2003) 28.
70 Cf. Assländer/Schumann (2011) 185 f.

(2) The investor postulates the normative superiority of the morally justified goals and strives to subordinate the financial goals to the morally justified ones. In this case, the scope of solutions for financial decisions is limited by the moral imperative.

In practical terms, financial and moral claims are likely to compete for redemption for most investors, as reflected by the magic square. The question often only becomes problematic when financially unprofitable or morally unacceptable decisions are at hand.[71]

The behavioural finance approach of recent capital market theory, however, shows that even in the case of financially unprofitable decisions, ethically motivated investors do not necessarily behave economically and rationally.[72] Human action in the individual investment of money is not only oriented towards maximising personal economic self-interest, but is also influenced by moral values and norms, even if it is financially disadvantageous. CENGIZ ET AL. justify this empirical observation with reference to FESTINGER's psychological theory of cognitive dissonance and the investor's desire for a clear conscience.

> "We believe that private investors are increasingly aware of the dilemma of benefiting from business practices that are inconsistent with their personal beliefs, not in the least because of the improved flow of information through the media. Ethical investments are therefore also a vehicle for resolving cognitive dissonances among investors ...."[73]

In order to weigh up the financial returns of an investment against the moral responsibility of the use of funds, however, the investor at the least needs key data on both variables. The financial return of ethical investments has

71 Cf. Assländer/Schumann (2011) 186 on this fundamental conflict in the relationship between superordination and subordination between economic objectives and ethical objectives. Interesting in this context is Schaefers (2017) 227–230 and Gabriel (2017) 65–68. These authors make a typological distinction between economistic, morally compliant and supererogatory investors and – correspondingly – economistic, morally compliant and supererogatorally acting investment advisors.

72 Cf. Kahnemann/Tversky (1979); Fünfgeld (2009) 1.

73 Cengiz et al. (2010) 263, translated by the author [MS]; on the role of Festinger's concept of cognitive dissonance in the context of business ethics see also Neuhäuser (2011) 80–83.

been empirically investigated in various studies and will be discussed in the following. The moral acceptance of the use of funds, on the other hand, depends on the adherence to the underlying moral values and norms. It is discussed in more detail in Chapter 3 on the basis of the criteria of ethical investments.

2.3.2 Lower return (underperformance) as a test case for morally justified investments

The effect of ethical investing on the return of an investment is controversial.[74] The question under discussion is whether – as described above – there really is a conflict between financial objectives and the ethical responsibility of the use of funds, or whether these objectives are actually compatible. In empirical studies, three results and lines of argumentation can be found.

(1) Excess return on ethical investments through technological and social advantage

These studies show that ethical investments are more profitable than conventional investments. A company's conduct that is based on moral criteria therefore goes hand in hand with numerous competitive advantages: More professional, long-term management, above-average reputation and trust among investors, more sustainable, innovative technologies, and better social relations with relevant stakeholders (e.g., employees, communities, suppliers) are cited as success factors that contribute to lower costs, higher sales prices or a lower risk and ultimately, to a better return.[75]

Financial intermediaries who benefit from selling ethical financial products often use this argument in favour of ethical investment. Ideationally motivated interest groups who promote ethical financial investments out of a moral conviction and at the same time want to use the power of economic arguments may raise this claim, too.

---

74 Cf. the studies by Pinner (2003) 36 ff and 50 ff; Schröder (2008) 519 ff, Fricke (2010) 64 f and Schneeweiss (2002) 125–129.

75 Cf. Pennekamp (2012) 1 f and the references given therein. For a critical comparison of the performance of such studies cf. Assländer/Schenkel (2009) 49 f.

(2) Average return and lack of significance of financial effect

These studies show no significant difference in return between ethical investments and conventional investments. They argue that compliance with moral criteria cannot be meaningfully isolated in the context of corporate behaviour and that the impact on a company's success cannot be clearly captured and may even be negligible.[76] Different forms of this line of argumentation are used by proponents as well as by sceptics of ethical investing.

(3) Lower return (underperformance) due to cost of moral restraint

These studies show a lower return on ethical investments compared to conventional investments. According to this argumentation, the consistent observance of moral criteria in the economic activity of companies primarily leads to additional financial expenses compared to those competitors who exploit the moral grey areas of legal action selfishly and opportunistically to maximise returns. In addition, ethical investing limits the investor's ability to diversify his investments because he can no longer choose from all the available forms of investment. This potentially increases the risk of his investment.[77]

The argumentation for a lower return is more likely represented by ethically motivated interest groups, which advocate *for* ethical investments, *despite* their financial disadvantages for the investor. With this argumentation they affirm their claim to sincerity and veracity in the implementation of moral criteria for the use of funds.[78]

Interim conclusion

Good reasons can be found for each of the above-mentioned arguments. The different results of the empirical studies can be traced back to the chosen methodology of performance comparisons, which is a point of contention in all forms of performance comparisons. For the present study, a clear statement is not of further relevance here in the sense that only the third case seems worth investigating from an ethical point of view.

---

76 Cf. Herger (2019) 29.

77 Cf. Cengiz et al. (2010) 263; Pennekamp (2012) 1 f; Jahn-Madell (2009) 387. Cf. also Beck/Layes (2017) 99–113 on risk-adjusted returns on ethical investments from the perspective of capital market research and portfolio theory.

78 Cf. e.g. Arbeitsgruppe DBK (2010) 34.

Only in the case in which a genuine tension exists between financial and moral goals of the investment does the question about the moral justifiability of an investment actually become problematic for the investor and thus also relevant for the ethical reflection. In the other two cases described, it can be plausibly argued that a reasonable investor will prefer to choose an ethical investment over a conventional investment if it is financially more attractive or at least equally profitable. In this case, he will act out of inclination and not necessarily out of responsibility.

At this point, however, it should be emphasised that it is always a fundamental goal of ethical investing to achieve a positive return. This means that the invested financial capital should be maintained or increased in value. By definition, this distinguishes investments from other uses of funds, such as donations, where the donor is not looking for a financial benefit.[79]

The above-mentioned impact investing represents a borderline case here as it explicitly takes into account elements of a non-financially oriented philanthropic approach, i.e., it does not always aim to achieve a positive financial return. Today, investors of this form of ethical investing therefore explicitly differentiate between two variants of impact investing, which are referred to as "Finance First" (a positive return is sought) and "Impact First" (a positive return is subordinated to a defined effect).[80]

But then how can the investor find a morally justifiable balance if a tension between financial and moral criteria is assumed? The concrete moral criteria of investment, which are discussed in Chapter 3 and their normative status play a decisive role in answering this question.

In purely practical terms, however, only in a few cases will the investor actually make the effort to analyse and reflect in depth on the moral criteria of his investment, as the present study aims to do. In practice, in this case he can orientate himself on a selection of guidebook literature that deals with questions of sustainable investment.

---

79 Cf. Gabriel (2008) 36.

80 Cf. Oehri (2012) 1. Regarding the special case of investments in microcredit and the balancing questions that arise in this context, cf. Stüttgen (2019a) 117 ff.

2.4 Normative guidance on ethical investing

In line with the demand for ethically justified investment opportunities, not only the range of ethically labelled investment products is growing, but also the supply of written advice for investors. Depending on the author and content, two types of orientation aids can be roughly distinguished: The first type of orientation support are more conventional money advisors with a focus on ethical investing as a trending topic. Authors are mostly active or former players in the financial services industry. The second type of orientation aid can be described as informative guides with a moral claim. Authors are usually interest groups, associations, foundations or churches that seek to sensitise selected target groups to the connections and backgrounds of ethical investments for moral reasons.

Both types of orientation aids share the basic assumption that investment activities are part of the investor's personal area of responsibility. The interpretation of this assumption and ultimately of the concept of responsibility, however, differs in each case. While the more conventional investment advisors appeal to the investor's responsibility to take optimal care of his own finances, the more enlightening guides interpret the investor's personal responsibility as his co-responsibility with regard to the moral close as well as distant effects of an investment in an interconnected world.

2.4.1 Conventional investment advice with ethics as a trending topic in finance

The orientation aids referred to here as "conventional financial advisors with an ethical focus" are based on the assumption that ethical investment pays off in the long term. In this respect, they build on the assumption presented in the previous subchapter that ethical investing can achieve a relative excess return or is at least as profitable as a conventional investment, but less risky.

To answer the question of how an investor should behave in real conflicts between a morally unacceptable economic activity and financial goals, these guidebooks make no real contribution. At least, however, they include certain thoughts about the moral responsibility of the use of funds in considerations about financial investments.

In the German-speaking countries, books with titles such as "How to make a profit while improving the world"[81], "Ethical Investments. Returns with 'clean' funds"[82], "Successfully investing in green investments. Ecological – ethical – sustainable"[83], or "Green money. The Handbook for Ethical-Ecological Investments 2012/2013"[84] can be mentioned here as examples.

This type of written guidance sensitises a larger number of investors to the topic of ethical investing and thus helps to guide it out of countries in which it is still a small niche. This can be seen as an advantage of these publications.

However, it must be critically assessed that the label of ethics in this form of advice is often misused or at least used in a misleading way. This weakens the core idea of ethical investing. Strictly speaking, this is not as much a problem of the written advice in itself, rather than that of a financial services industry that has recently discovered the label of ethics in a marketing-oriented sense as a seal of quality, exploited for its own purposes and for the sale of investment products, thereby undermining its content. The corresponding written guidance, which blindly adopts this approach, must therefore be regarded as rather questionable, or at least ambivalent, as an orientation aid for the investor.

2.4.2 Informative guides with normative moral standards

On the other side of the spectrum of orientation aids are the publications described here as "informative guides". They mostly come from idealistic and not financially motivated interest groups, associations, foundations or the Catholic and Protestant churches.

The most differentiated and influential orientation aid in German-speaking countries is the *Frankfurt-Hohenheim Guidelines (FHG)*. It is aimed at investors, rating agencies, fund providers, banks, companies, and other interest groups and formulates ethical criteria for the evaluation

81 Schwanfelder (2012), title translated by the author [MS].
82 Pinner (2003), title translated by the author [MS].
83 Rotthaus (2009), title translated by the author [MS].
84 Deml/Blisse (2011), title translated by the author [MS].

of companies. The FHG was developed by a scientific working group of ethicists and economists in cooperation with companies and rating agencies from Germany and Switzerland. The opportunities and challenges of this approach to investor orientation are explored in more detail in Chapter 3.[85]

Other guidelines from interest groups, associations or foundations are either aligned to the FHG or expand on special focus topics. The "Guideline for Ethically Oriented Investors"[86] from CRIC, the Association for the Promotion of Ethics and Sustainability in Investments, the "Development Policy Criteria in Ethical Investment"[87] from the SÜDWIND INSTITUTE and various guidelines and publications from the FORUM NACHHALTIGE GELDANLAGEN, an association of institutions (non-governmental organisations, banks, and specialist institutions) that are interested in ethical investments, are particularly worth mentioning here.[88]

The two major churches in Switzerland and Germany have also published guidelines on ethical investment on various occasions, mostly as grey literature or as writings and presentations on the Internet. The following guidelines are just a few examples: "How to invest money responsibly? Initiatives to the discussion about church investments"[89], "Ethical Investment – Taking Responsibility with Investments!"[90], "Change the world with investments? A guide to ethical investment"[91], "Guide to sustainable investments in church households"[92] and "Guide to ethically sustainable investments in the Protestant church"[93].

What these writings have in common is that they are both explicative and appellative in character. They orient themselves towards partially differing collections of criteria for ethical investing, but at the same time ask their readers to independently identify and reflect on ethical criteria when investing money, in order to allow this reflection to flow into their

85 Cf. Hoffmann/Ott/Scherhorn (1997), 9 f and 21.
86 Cf. CRIC (2008), title translated by the author [MS].
87 Cf. Schneeweiss (2009), title translated by the author [MS].
88 Cf. FNG (2013).
89 Justitia et Pax (1989), title translated by the author [MS].
90 ZDK (2007), title translated by the author [MS].
91 Arbeitsgruppe DBK (2010), title translated by the author [MS].
92 Ev. Kirche von Westfalen (2006), title translated by the author [MS].
93 EKD (2013), title translated by the author [MS].

own investment decisions.[94] Thus these guides are based on a more scientific and reflective understanding of ethics.

2.4.3 Appeals to practical reason and moral obligation

There is no clear line dividing the two ideal types of guidance for the ethical investor outlined above. The most reliable way to draw a distinction is to see whether a guide primarily positions ethics as a lucrative trending topic, or whether it appeals to the moral obligation of the investor to assume social and environmental responsibility towards his fellow human beings and his environment, even if the investment approach may reduce the return on investment.

The interdependency of these two trains of thought is further deepened from a theoretical point of view in Chapter 3. For this purpose, not only the moral criteria for assessing companies as objects of investment are reflected (Sections 3.2 and 3.3), but also the normative status of an investment transaction itself (Section 3.4). Finally, the question of weighing up normative conflicts is discussed (Chapter 4). Before doing so, a brief interim conclusion of the previous considerations should be drawn.

2.5 Interim conclusion

Based on our considerations so far, the opportunities and challenges of a moral justification of investments can be summarized as follows.

(1) An analysis must be based on the concept of "ethical investing" itself. This term is very broad both in theory and in practice. For pragmatic reasons, it makes sense to share this broad understanding of the term. However, a broad and thus ultimately blurred understanding of this term in itself represents an opportunity as well as a challenge to the moral justification of financial investments.
The opportunity posed by a vaguely and broadly defined term lies in the fact that it makes it possible to introduce ethical reflections into the discourses of the financial services industry. A broad term has

94 Cf. Justitia et Pax (1989) 3 f; ZDK (2007) 3 f; Arbeitsgruppe DBK (2010) 34; Evangelische Kirche von Westfalen (2006) 18; EKD (2013) 7.

the potential to sensitise a wide audience of financial investors and intermediaries to ethical issues. Thus, for example, the moral responsibility of shareholders or injustice in the distribution of rights of the production factors capital on the one hand, and labour or nature on the other hand, can be put up for discussion and left to practical reason for reflection. As a collective, reflection and bridging concept, a broad understanding of ethical investing can stimulate the dialogue between different professions (e.g., fund providers, church representatives, authors of guidebook literature) and scientific theories and thus raise the level of ethical reflection in economic contexts. In this way, moral norms and values in the financial services industry, economy, and society can potentially be strengthened.

The downside and serious challenge posed by a broad concept of ethical investing, however, is that the concept of ethics is potentially used meaninglessly. Well-founded systematic approaches to applied ethics then no longer stand out amongst the noise. Financial market players (e.g., banks, funds, rating agencies) can misuse the concept of ethics for their own means and in an inflationary manner due to its vagueness and lack of legal protection. The attempt to morally reflect and justify the phenomenon of investment then runs the practical risk of being misunderstood as a trend or marketing gag in a confusion of concepts that is difficult to understand.

A vague and inconsistent concept of ethical investing also creates the practical issue that financial products and providers that claim to invest "ethically" are no longer comparable due to a lack of binding standards for a private investor, potentially creating confusion and overstretching the moral capacity of the investor.

(2) The concept of "ethical investing" assumes a causal relationship between the investment activity of an investor and the moral conduct of the invested companies. This alleged causal connection is seen as both an opportunity and a challenge to the moral justification of financial investments.

An opportunity for morally justified investment actions is constituted by the fact that one can plausibly reconstruct a causal connection between an investor's investment and the moral conduct of companies. This causal connection, which is important for our chain of argumentation, can be empirically and historically validated. It has recently gained further plausibility due to the growing level of transparency through digital media and an increasing range of different products and providers of ethical investments.

In practice, ethical investing can have a positive effect on the moral actions of objects of investment. In addition, ethical investing can also have an impact on the investor himself by reflecting on his investment criteria and further developing his moral judgement. This can also constitute an opportunity for a morally justified investment.

But the argument about the causal connections of ethical investing in the efficiency of influencing an investor on an object of investment is also challenged. In practice, the effect of an investor's influence on the moral conduct of investment objects is reduced, for example, by information asymmetries and control issues (principal-agency problem). This observation is likely to weaken the argument for the moral justification of investments solely for factual reasons.

(3) Ethical investing is based on the assumption that individual investors do not optimise their financial investments in an exclusively rational way. i.e., according to economic aspects. More recent approaches to behavioural finance argue that investors can incorporate non-economic criteria – moral as well as non-moral criteria – into their investment decisions.

Here, applied ethics offers the *opportunity* to tie in with economic insights into the individual decision-making behaviour of investors and to argue using these insights. Applied ethics also has the opportunity to increasingly connect its findings to sector-specific scientific insights and to increase ethical reflection. In contrast to its historical precursors of "faith consistent investing", which referred to truths of faith and revelation in their argumentation, it can weigh up and discuss arguments in relation to reason.

The proposition of normative guidelines for specific investment decisions, however, also has its limit. In particular, weighing up moral and financial investment criteria poses a challenge. First, it consists of identifying and convincingly justifying moral criteria for investment – i.e., the evaluation criteria of objects of investment. Second, the challenge is to provide reliable standards for weighing up moral and financial criteria in decision-making situations with conflicting goals and to justify their normative status. This challenge will be examined in the following from the point of view of ethical theory.

3 Justification of moral criteria for investing

In Chapter 2 we analysed the factual challenges of ethical investing. Chapter 3 builds on these ideas and looks at the normative criteria that ethical investing can and *should* be guided by. As a first step, we are reviewing a very comprehensive collection of criteria for assessing the moral conduct of companies – the FHG. In a second step, we then deal with selected problems of the justification of standards for ethical investing, as well as the implementation of ethical standards in the investment process.

3.1 Justification of standards in applied ethics

The task of applied ethics is to apply normative rules and principles to specific issue in order to assess them from a moral point of view or to shape corresponding spheres of action morally. For such an application, in a first step, rules and principles must be identified that fit individual cases and case types. Second, not only must these rules and principles be explicitly justified, but also the mediating bridging elements that link the principles to an analysed case.[95] The justification must legitimise itself through moral-philosophical, reason-based procedures; it cannot prove itself solely through the normative power of the objective or subjective judgements of value.

In the present study, however, such an approach to applied ethics faces a number of challenges. There are numerous guidebooks with practical investment recommendations on ethical investing. However, there are few relevant principles and rules for the moral orientation of private investors that are both systematic and application-specific. Where such principles and rules exist, they often have certain weaknesses, e.g., in their normative binding character, their application or with regard to important bridging elements, which could offer private investors a practical orientation for making their decisions.

In this situation, the present study seeks to mediate between ethical theory and its explanatory procedures on the one hand, and their practical application in private investment on the other. To this end, the power of

95 Cf. Thurnherr (2010) 8 and 21.

various theoretical approaches (e.g., utilitarian ethics, [pluralistic] deontological ethics, supererogation) will be used. These ethical theories will help to critically reflect on moral criteria with regard to their application in the context of ethical investment.

However, this procedure is systematically demanding in that it involves the application of different ethical theories at different points of the investigation. Different ethical theories are thus not directly compared with each other at each point of the investigation. This must be remembered in the course of the further investigation.

Thus, the construction of the FHG is based on a preference-utilitarian ethic as a background theory. The subject area of this guide is the assessment of the actions of companies according to moral criteria.

Deontological or supererogatory ethics is the basis for the following discussion as to whether – and if so, how – a possible positive obligation to ethical investing could be justified. The subject area of the investigation here is the investment activity of the individual investor.

Finally, principles of pluralistic deontological ethics are used to introduce assessment categories that could assist an investor in making investment decisions in areas of conflicting norms. These thoughts are complemented by additional principles of a moral-philosophical tradition that are directly related to the practice of ethical investing. In this specific context, however, mapping an ethical theory onto the principles reviewed becomes increasingly challenging.

With regard to this approach, utilitarian ethics on the one hand and deontological ethics on the other hand will be introduced as two important schools of thought in normative ethics. They differ significantly in the way in which moral judgements shall be justified. Utilitarian ethics essentially justifies moral judgements in a consequentialist manner, i.e., with reference to the consequences of action, whereas deontological ethics justifies them by referring to the inherent legitimacy or illegitimacy of an action itself.[96]

96 Cf. Werner (2011b) 3–8 and Birnbacher (2013) 115 f. Birnbacher describes consequentialist-teleological ethics as a counter-concept to deontological ethics. This type of systematic juxtaposition is often found in literature, but it is not always used uniformly. In the present study, utilitarianism as a form of a consequentialist-teleological ethics is contrasted with deontology.

3.1.1 Utilitarian ethics

Utilitarianism is an ethics of principles, the supreme principle of which is the principle of maximising utility. In classical utilitarianism, the concept of utility is understood as the sum of happiness, i.e., the subjective sense of pleasure, of all sentient beings. The moral principle of utilitarianism consists in the realisation of "the greatest happiness". In utilitarianism as a consequentialist-teleological ethic, actions are never "in themselves" good or bad, but they are always evaluated with regard to the consequences of the action or their contribution to increasing the overall benefit.[97]

Utilitarianism is based on three pillars:

(1) *The principle of consequences*: The criterion for the moral correctness of an action is exclusively its consequences;
(2) *The theory of value*: It assigns values to a criterion, on the basis of which the consequences and thus the benefit of an action are evaluated;
(3) *The principle of summation/maximisation*: The sole point of view for the evaluation is the collective total benefit, i.e., the total benefit of all those affected by an action. An action is considered morally correct if it increases the overall collective benefit more than alternative actions.[98]

In contrast to classical utilitarianism, preference utilitarianism does not demand the maximisation of subjectively felt happiness, but the maximisation of the satisfaction of the preferences of those affected.[99] "An action that opposes the preference of any being without this preference being balanced by opposing preferences is morally wrong."[100] Preference utilitarianism forms the background theory of the methodology of the FHG, which seeks to morally evaluate the actions of companies as objects of investment in its subject area.

97 Cf. Werner (2011b) 5 f.
98 Cf. Ricken (2003) 276.
99 Cf. Werner (2011a) 8.
100 Singer (1993) 128 f, cited from Ricken (2003) 277, translated by the author [MS].

3.1.2 Deontological ethics

Deontological ethics derives its name from the Greek term "to deon" (the obliging, the intended).[101] Deontological, i.e., ethical theories concerning the doctrine of duties, judge actions according to a scheme of the following type: "Actions of the type h are always right (or wrong) in situations of the types, regardless of their consequences."[102]

Deontological ethics attempts to justify norms with regard to the inner nature of an action and not (primarily) with regard to the moral or non-moral quality of its consequences. In deontological ethics, some actions considered to be morally good, have an independent or intrinsic value (e.g., keeping contracts, not lying), compliance with certain moral principles is considered to be valuable in itself. Because certain forms of morally correct actions possess an intrinsic value independent of consequences, they are not only means, but at least partially also ends in themselves.[103]

According to HORSTER, the starting point of deontology can be found in Kantian philosophy. According to KANT, a maxim for action only has a moral value when a person acts out of duty. To act out of duty means that one acts guided by a maxim like the categorical imperative, which should direct behaviour without any deviation.[104] With regard to duties, KANT distinguishes between perfect duties, which must be fulfilled at all costs, and imperfect duties, the fulfilment of which is meritorious.[105] Ethical investing is likely to be assigned to a particular category of imperfect duties.[106] In the form of charitable obligations or positive obligations, the binding nature of these obligations with regard to the matter of the individual act of an investor will be discussed over the course of this study.

DAVID ROSS has shown that moral duties must not necessarily be based on a single principle – as in KANT's case on the categorical imperative. ROSS also examined the issue relevant to our investigation, as to which

101 Cf. Horster (2012) 44.
102 Broads (1930), cited from Birnbacher (2013) 113, translated by the author [MS].
103 Cf. Birnbacher (2013) 113–119.
104 Cf. Horster (2012) 45.
105 Cf. Mieth (2012) 74 f.
106 Cf. Ott (1997) 218 f.

principles allow to balance out between conflicting moral duties in concrete applications. His approach is understood as a pluralistic deontology and as a material ethics of duty with a pronounced teleological impact. Ross's approach is based on a number of selected duties,[107] so-called "prima facie duties" (=conditional duties, assessment principles), which are intended to provide guidance for judging in a situation of normative conflict. The approach has a heuristic potential to lead the way in contexts of ethical investment decisions. It can theoretically mediate between a strict deontology and a utilitarian approach by helping to balance the strengths and weaknesses of these approaches.[108]

The following description provides an overview of the objects of analysis, theoretical approaches to justification and the conceptual categories in a first step, and then the explanations, which are based on them in a second step.

3.2 Criteria of the Frankfurt-Hohenheim Guidelines (FHG) to assess a company's moral conduct

Ethical investing requires criteria that distinguish it from conventional investing. These criteria are first captured here in the morally founded norms and values according to which companies or their leaders act. As already explained, a private investor in his role as a shareholder and thus co-owner, has a moral co-responsibility for the entrepreneurial action of his objects of investment.

But what moral criteria can and *should* an investor use to orientate him- or herself in this situation? How can these criteria be justified and what moral obligation can be derived from them for the investor?

These key questions will be examined below. To this end, the FHG will be analysed in a first step. It is the most comprehensive and at the same time most influential criteria handbook for ethical investing in German-speaking countries.[109]

107 In contrast to Kant, Ross is understood as a material ethicist whose theory is based on a model of Aristotelian ethics. Cf. Birnbacher/Hoerster (1976) 231 and Birnbacher (2013) 159.

108 Cf. Horster (2012) 47 f.

109 Cf. Hoffmann/Ott/Scherhorn (1997); Hoffmann/Scherhorn (2002) 39 f and 52–56.

Objects of analysis	*Theoretical approach to justification*	*Conceptual categories*	*Category and subject of the judgment*
Criteria for the action of companies as objects of investment (Sections 3.2 and 3.3)	*Preference utilitarian ethics* (FHG)	Values; goods; benefits; harm	Moral and evaluative (axiological) judgements of value on the consequences of an action
Investment decisions of investors (Section 3.4)	*Deontological ethics* (KANT; MIETH); *Supererogation* (URMSON; MIETH)	Imperfect duty: Charitable duty , positive duty; supererogatory acts	Moral judgements of actions; moral judgments of value on the motives of an action
Considerations by investors in situations of normative conflict (Chapter 4)	*Pluralistic deontological ethics* (ROSS) *Applied Ethics* (GABRIEL/ SCHLAGNITWEIT)	Prima facie duties: Non-maleficence, beneficence, justice, self-improvement Mid-level rules: Minimizing harm; consideration of goods, etc.	Actions (and consequences of actions); "Mixed" objective and moral judgment

Figure 4: Objects and theoretical justification approaches for financial investments. Own presentation based on Birnbacher (2013) 49.

The FHG is a collection – a catalogue – of ethical criteria to assess a company's behaviour. It is theoretically and methodologically justified and highly differentiated. The FHG is intended to serve a broad target group – private and institutional investors as well as financial institutions and rating agencies – as an orientation aid for the selection, evaluation, and rating of ethical investments.[110]

The FHG distinguishes between, first, the "criteriological basis" of the rating of companies, second, the "rating" itself as an assessment practice

110 Cf. Hoffmann/Scherhorn (2002) 39 f.

based on the criteria and, thirdly, the "ethical investing" as a financial activity that can be based on criteria and rating. Of these three elements, the "criteriological basis" for company valuation represents the core and main concern of the guideline.[111]

The authors HOFFMANN/OTT/SCHERHORN describe the objectives of the guide as follows.

> "Overall, we expect a development on the capital markets in which investment decisions will increasingly be made from a moral point of view. We also assume that there is a market segment with growing demand for such investments to which the provider side (banks, investment companies) has not yet responded adequately. ... It is quite important to us to influence capital flows for moral reasons in order to make normative knowledge ... applicable in this way. "[112]

The FHG has been well received in practice by investors, financial institutions and rating agencies since its appearance in 1997. It has also been further developed into other formats and practical applications and is now regarded as an important standard of ethical investment.[113] In 2004 already, more than 1,000 companies were assessed for their compliance with environmental, social, and cultural criteria and assets of around one billion euros were managed in German-speaking countries according to the criteria of the FHG.[114] This justifies a more detailed examination of the objective, criteria, methodology, and theoretical assumptions of the FHG. For the purposes of this study, the focus is not laid on a detailed discussion of all the criteria of the FHG. For our purpose, the theoretical considerations underlying the selection and justification of its criteria are more important. In order to be able to reflect on these considerations, it shall first be illustrated how the FHG is structured theoretically and methodologically and how it should be applied from the point of view of its authors.

---

111 Cf. Ott (1997) 221.

112 Hoffmann/Ott/Scherhorn (1997) 14, translated by the author [MS].

113 Cf. Gabriel (2008) 34; Berg (2011) 313.

114 Cf. Hoffmann (2004) 21.

3.2.1 Environmental, social, and cultural compatibility as the top criteria

At the highest level, the FHG comprises of the three main criteria of the environmental compatibility, social compatibility, and cultural compatibility of economic activity. Depending on the context, these criteria are not always uniformly referred to as norms or values. None of the three criteria follow a simple definition, but are described in detail, explained theoretically, determined systematically and presented using the so-called value tree method, and differentiated in detailed lists with a total of around 850 individual criteria.[115]

Example: Under the criterion "cultural compatibility" you will find, among other things, GERT's norm "You shall not cause or inflict pain!" This standard is broken down into various sub-criteria, e.g., into the question "Does the company tolerate heavy child labour (modern slaves)?"[116].

The user may determine the list of criteria to be applied to the object of assessment. Typically, the object of assessment is a company or a company-related area of action in which an investment is to be made. In principle, however, whole countries or other units can be defined as the object of investigation.[117]

The overriding values of the collection of criteria are the long-term bio-survival and intergenerational humane living conditions for all people. The co-authors HOFFMANN/SCHERHORN write about this.

> "[T]he overall concept with the triad of assessment criteria ... [together with the] rating methodology, the approach offers ethically oriented investors of very different origins, traditions, and cultures a good opportunity for commitment, because everyone can identify with it with their subjective perception of values. This is quite plausible when one considers that the central concern, both in terms of criteria and the rating concept, is biosafety for all. It is nothing more than a matter of guaranteeing and safeguarding a humane way of life for all human beings and of preserving the natural basis of life for present and future generations. Who would not be able to affirm this principle both from the perspective of one's own culture and from the perspective of another culture and religion?"[118]

---

115 Cf. Hoffmann/Ott/Scherhorn (1997) 16 f and 27–205; Hoffmann/Scherhorn (2002) 39 and 79–109.

116 Hoffmann/Ott/Scherhorn (1997) 96 f, 196 f.

117 Cf. Hoffmann/Ott/Scherhorn (1997) 17; Hoffmann/Scherhorn (2002) 83–87.

118 Hoffmann/Scherhorn (2002) 40, translated by the author [MS].

The aim of the value tree analysis is to strengthen moral and evaluative (axiological) criteria against the dominance of economic and technical criteria (profitability, efficiency) of economic activity.[119] In this respect, the FHG is a supplement to financial evaluation criteria and ratings, while it does not integrate the latter into the method itself and merely calls to be used as a complementary instrument to these financial methods, ratios, and evaluation instruments.

3.2.2 Reconstruction of moral criteria via discourse and consensus

In order to be able to present the guide's criteria as exhaustively and logically consistent as possible, first, existing social norms (behavioural expectations) and values (desirability) are reconstructed. In the next step, norms and values, duties and preferences are then – albeit not always consistently – conceptually abstracted and only referred to as preferences or values.[120]

In the "cultural compatibility" dimension, the FHG refers, for example, to the basic moral norms of Bernhard Gert, in order to identify the core set of moral principles.[121] For other criteria, other values or norms considered fundamental are used, on which, from the authors' point of view, there is a broad and cross-cultural/cross-country consensus[122]. Despite its claim to consensus, consistency, and completeness, the collection of norms and values created in this way is, however, subject to the fundamental reservation that it is fallible and improvable.[123]

The FHG assumes a descriptive and not a normative ethics. It claims to provide a collection of standards and values that is as comprehensive as

119 Cf. Hoffmann/Ott/Scherhorn (1997) 15.
120 Cf. Ott (1997) 223 and 233 ff.
121 Cf. Ott (1997) 223 with reference to Gert (1983).
122 Cf. to a methodically similar procedure in the derivation of criteria for ethical investing Schneeweiss (1998) 85–88 with reference to the catalogue of values of the project "Weltethos". Basic catalogues of standards can also be found in Hoffmann/Scherhorn (2002) 30 f, which refer to the ecological Valdez principles and the socially oriented Sullivan principles, and in Pinner (2003) 92 f, which refers to the guiding principles of the UN Global Compact initiative.
123 Cf. Ott (1997) 235.

possible for morally justified investments in companies.[124] Nevertheless, the FHG must not be misunderstood or misinterpreted as being based on an understanding that ethics is simply a comprehensive collection of moral norms and values. The authors of the FHG explicitly reject such an understanding.

The value tree method on which the FHG is based assumes value pluralism as a social fact and strives to include all social groups and their legitimate interests in the method. In this sense, it is conceived, at least from its intention, as an integrative-discursive procedure of justifying moral criteria. The authors emphasise that the proposed collection of values should serve the user for reflection, be capable of development and ideally arise from a discursive procedure of justification or should be applied in such a procedure. They then limit this postulate to the derivation of the FHG and explain that for pragmatic reasons, the postulate was developed in a small working group.[125]

Systematically and ethically, the methodology of the FHG is based on a preference-utilitarian axiology which, according to the authors, need not be shared in its application, but which, according to them, is methodologically useful.[126]

3.2.3 Assessment, weighting, and rating of criteria by investors

The FHG aims to provide a template for a rating agency, a financial institution or an investor to search for criteria in comparing morally justified investment opportunities. On the basis of the list of criteria of the FHG, a reflexive and discursive process of justification and application of moral criteria is to be initiated, which includes all the legitimate interests of the stakeholders. The purpose of the FHG is therefore not to complete the reflection process of an investor or rating agency, albeit still considered a necessary step. Ott comments on this.

> "In view of the difference between the possibilities of 'ethical investment' and the individual subject, the guideline serves as orientation; however, it does not spare the investors of any independent value decisions by which this difference is closed

---

124 Cf. Ott (1997) 226 and 234 f.
125 Cf. Ott (1997) 226, 230–232 and 234.
126 Cf. Ott (1997) 230–232 and 227.

> in different ways. ... We assume ... that the clientele of the EÖR [MS: Ethical-Ecological Rating] is largely composed of persons who have a formal meta-preference for autonomously determining and weighting their value preferences. ... This assumption is based on an assumed internal connection between a) the morally motivated basic decision of 'ethical investment' and b) the interest in self-determined decisions."[127]

The FHG therefore offers a detailed collection of moral criteria which are worth considering and which are – more or less – theoretically justified. How these criteria are applied in practice is left to the judgement of the user. The latter can use the FHG to select criteria, to evaluate the respective fulfilment of individual criteria on the basis of a correspondingly defined scale, in order to finally combine these individual evaluations in an overall assessment, a rating, for the analysed company. Figure 5 gives an overview of the dimensions to be assessed in the overall rating.

As an intermediate step in the rating process, the user must weight the criteria. This weighting depends on his preference structure and is not specified in the method itself. This means that in principle the fulfilment of individual criteria can be offset by other criteria. This is a consequence of the consequentialist approach of the FHG. In order to exclude morally unacceptable consequences by compensating between values, it is recommended to define knockout criteria on the basis of moral norms. Though the authors identify the question of who defines these types of moral norms and what these criteria should be as an issue to be addressed, they deliberately leave it open due to the assumed pluralism of values.[128]

By selecting the criteria, their evaluation and their weighting, the user determines a rating that finally indicates, either as a whole or broken down into sub-criteria, how well or poorly the company in question fulfils the moral criteria of the FHG. The rating can also be used to show the relative position of a company compared to competitors in the same industry. If there is a certain level of transparency between companies, it can ideally contribute to competition between companies for better ethical ratings.

127 Ott (1997) 253 f, translated by the author [MS].

128 Cf. Hoffmann/Ott/Scherhorn (1997) 249 f and 242 f. Weighing up between financial criteria of investment on the one hand and moral criteria on the other hand – as was worked out as a problem in Chapter 2 – is neither applied nor aimed at in the methodical design of the FHG.

Overall rating of the company's responsibility					
Social and cultural rating			Environmental rating		
External stakeholders	Staff	Management	Environmental management	Products/services	Environmental data
• Suppliers, customers, etc. • Government, community • Foreign countries, cultural adaptation • Damaged persons • Economic relationships	• Co-determination, employee development • Working hours, remuneration • Workplace safety, health • …	• Corporate mission and goals • Representatives • Audits, reporting	• Goals, representatives • Eco-balance sheet, controlling, reporting • Standards abroad, cooperations • Training, office environment, procurement	• Product and service development measures, e.g., longevity, reduction of consumption and emissions, avoidance of environmentally harmful materials	• Waste generation and composition • Energy and water consumption • Pollutants in sewage • Emissions in the air

Figure 5: Rating of companies in the Frankfurt-Hohenheim approach. Cf. Hoffmann/Scherhorn (2002) 102 f.

According to the authors of the guideline, one of the strengths of the FHG lies precisely in this type of use. In contrast to a pure negative selection of companies based on moral exclusion criteria, the FHG enables the evaluation of strengths and weaknesses of a company compared to the best and worst competitors in an industry. Thus, the application of the guideline potentially contributes to the fact that companies not only measure themselves against each other according to economic criteria, but increasingly also according to morally justified criteria and in striving for specific improvements.[129]

3.3 The limited binding force of moral criteria as another key challenge

The FHG aims to provide investors with an orientation aid in the moral assessment of companies as objects of investment. For this purpose, it proposes a distribution of roles and responsibilities between the expert group of ethicists who should propose lists of criteria on the one hand, and its users on the other. The latter should select, assess, prioritise, and weight the proposed criteria in order to compare objects of investment.[130]

Due to its basic theoretical assumptions and its methodical structure, however, the interpretation and application of the FHG places high demands on the user and his ethical competence. Here, three problems are pointed out in particular. By indicating these issues, there is no intention to question the practical benefits of the FHG, which have proven themselves in many applications. Rather, they serve to further approach the question of which criteria of ethical investment a private investor can and *should* orientate himself by.

3.3.1 Limitations of basic theoretical and methodological assumptions

The FHG claims to be independent of ethical theories and to pursue theoretical minimalism. Ott elaborates on this.

---

129 Cf. Hoffmann/Scherhorn (2002) 101–107 and 41 f.
130 Cf. Ott (1997) 259.

> "As far as ethical theories are concerned, our guideline is independent of the dispute about ethical paradigms (ethics of goals, duties, virtues, values). The guide does not rest on a particular basic concept of ethics. We consider this to be an advantage in view of the theoretical competition in ethics. The guide should therefore be applicable for a Kantian as well as for a utilitarian, a contractualist, an ecocentric, a discourse ethicist, a representative of Christian social ethics or a communitarian. According to their conception of ethics and the resulting consequences, these persons will each set different accents in the hierarchical structure and prioritisation of values."[131]

However, the independence from any theory claimed here can be questioned critically for various reasons.

(1) The authors themselves categorise the FHG both theoretically and methodically several times, e.g., with regard to its preference-utilitarian methodology, with regard to its foundation in descriptive ethics or with regard to the intended discursive reasoning procedure.[132] From the author's [MS] perspective, these theoretical and methodological assumptions form, if not a normative, then at least a factually strong prejudice that will guide the moral orientation of the FHG user in practice in terms of content and process.

(2) The apparent independence of the FHG from theory shifts possible theoretical controversies to the application level, for example when it comes to weighting and considering criteria in the case of conflicts of interest within ethics. This sort of issues can ultimately only be resolved by referencing an ethical theory.
This is a challenge in the context of the FHG design in the sense that the definition of the morally relevant criteria is methodically assigned explicitly to the ethics experts, i.e., the authors of the guideline, and not to the user.[133] In fact, the latter should eventually adopt them – discursively, quasi-discursively or otherwise – by selecting, justifying and weighting them against each other. However, this process tends to

---

131 Ott (1997) 222, translated by the author [MS].

132 Cf. Ott (1997) 223–227.

133 Ulrich et al. (1998) 46 criticise the idea of such a distribution of roles between ethicists and those applying ethics with the argument that it assumes an immature user. However, the authors of the FHG point out on several occasions that they presuppose a sovereign, responsible user, so the criticism voiced by

be shortened, since the user can rely on an extensive collection of possible criteria to consider.

(3) In line with this theoretical boundary of the guide, a challenge arises from the fact that the FHG tries not to distinguish theoretically between duties and preferences, between moral norms and values. Due to the underlying preference-utilitarian method, duties and preferences are conceptually equal, without a claim to higher or lower importance. OTT sees less of a weakness in this approach, than the advantage of its openness to pluralistic values. He comments on this.

> "The VTA [MS: Value Tree Analysis] abstracts from the difference between duties and preferences and, since it only knows preferences, inevitably comes to the assumption that in principle all values can be offset by all others. But this problem ... could also ... be considered an advantage; for being categorically under-determined implies a great openness towards different values."[134]

The aforementioned characteristic of being categorically under-determined finally leads to the fact that the FHG as a collection of criteria does not give the user sufficient information on the moral obligation about any of the total of 850 individual criteria. Even those norms that can and *should* claim an unconditional binding force, such as human rights, are in fact considered equal to all other criteria in the FHG and to be considered.

ULRICH ET AL. criticise the danger of the arbitrary character of evaluation criteria which arises as the user is able to choose what suits him best.[135]

ASSLÄNDER and SCHENKEL also criticise the logic of a two-staged approach like the FHG (definition and selection of criteria) in another context with regard to the providers of ethical funds and their product design.

> "The compilation of the criteria becomes arbitrary in a way. It may then only orient itself towards the relevant wishes of the client and thus ultimately orient itself exclusively towards the demand behaviour of (potential) investors.

Ulrich et al. does not apply in this specific case. The present study criticises the proposed distribution of roles for other reasons. Academic ethicists delegate the solution of ethical issues to practitioners who, for practical reasons, are unable or at least unwilling to provide an ethical reflection comparable to that of the ethicists.

134 Ott (1997) 234, translated by the author [MS].

135 Cf. Ulrich/Jäger/Waxenberger (1998) 47.

> However, whether such a 'product' can then still be described as an 'ethics fund' seems questionable, at least from an ethical point of view. One would ultimately be dealing with an opportunistic concept of adaptation to more or less arbitrary, merely 'ethically' labelled 'customer wishes'. "[136]

According to ASSLÄNDER and SCHENKEL, ethical funds that follow an FHG-like methodology are not only arbitrarily definable, they can also hardly be compared with each other. The legally unprotected concept of ethics is thus potentially meaningless as a seal of quality, and the ethical fund landscape potentially becomes more opaque instead of becoming more transparent.[137]

3.3.2 Limitations of discursive justification in the derivation and application of moral criteria

One could also interpret the criteria of the FHG benevolently in a sense that they are initially still normatively under-determined, but that due to their discursive justification in the context of their application, they then potentially gain normative binding force.

Though this argument may seem theoretically plausible, it is unlikely to establish itself in practice. This is because, for pragmatic reasons, those defining the FHG, as scientifically rooted ethicists, already refrained from a discursive justification in the derivation of the criteria. It does not seem impossible, but at least unlikely, that the more practically and pragmatically oriented users – investors, financial institutions and rating agencies – are prepared to take an integrative and discursive path if it was already shortened in the theory for pragmatic reasons.

3.3.3 Limitations to the obligatory nature of specific norms and values

The theoretical and methodological design of the FHG implies that, despite its considerable range of values, the collection of criteria does not claim a

---

136 Assländer/Schenkel (2009) 53 with reference to Voigt/Kratochwil (2004) 316, translated by the author [MS].

137 Cf. Assländer/Schenkel (2009) 52–54. For the differentiation of ethical profiles of providers and consumers of ethical investments, cf. Scholand (2004) 122–130.

moral obligation, let alone an unconditional one, for any of these criteria. Instead, the decision of obligation is left to the user.

The user can indeed individually decide on the degree of commitment to moral norms, defining so-called knockout criteria according to personal values. These then specify the necessary conditions that a company must meet if it is to be considered at all for a morally justifiable investment. For example, a company that employs child labour, produces landmines or forces surgical sterilisation would no longer be eligible for investment. In the case of companies that violate one or more of these knockout criteria, the morally motivated investor should no longer invest his money, in order to avoid contradiction. Should the investor knowingly invest such a company, moral accusations can be made against him.[138]

According to OTT, potential candidates for such criteria – though not binding norms in the FHG – are human rights as well as BERNHARD GERT's moral rules.

> "Some basic knockout criteria (under weak premises) of Western humanism, some universal moral norms and human rights can be agreed upon; others will probably remain controversial. A company that actively participates in human rights abuses or subsidises a dictatorship would probably no longer be considered for an ethical investment. ... The candidates for knockout criteria are therefore primarily human rights and basic moral norms (Gert, 1983)."[139]

To use human rights and GERT's basic moral norms as universally binding moral norms for the FHG appears as one of various feasible and plausibly justifiable approaches. However, the fact that human rights and GERT's rules compete for binding force alongside many other criteria in the FHG's comprehensive collection of criteria poses a problem.

In another context, BIRNBACHER points out that GERT's rules are also slightly misleading due to their severity and rigidity and that this minimal ethical approach must necessarily be extremely tolerant due to its far-reaching claim with regard to possible exceptions.[140]

In the context of the concrete use in the FHG, however, due to their secondary order to a multitude of other norms the claim to binding force of

138 Cf. Ott (1997) 243.
139 Ott (1997) 248, translated by the author [MS].
140 Cf. Birnbacher (2013) 83 f.

these norms and human rights, appears to originate at a lower level than seems appropriate for these criteria from the author's point of view [MS]. As the large variety of criteria in the FHG provides an increased scope for interpretation and consideration of the binding force of human rights and GERT's moral rules, these ultimately lose their identity, which can be recognised in their acknowledged higher degree of moral certainty and binding force.

As a brief *interim conclusion,* it can be stated that the FHG makes far-reaching and in-depth considerations on the question as to which moral criteria can be used to assess ethical investments. However, when applying this approach, the degree to which the standards of ethical investment considered are ultimately binding remains open, which is perceived as unsatisfactory.

If the degree of commitment to moral norms to which the use of capital by companies is subject is not sufficiently defined, then ultimately the degree of commitment of ethical investing as a financial investment activity itself is also up for discussion, with the two being closely related. At least in this case the need for moral justification for a potential obligation of the investor to ethical investing is considerably increased.

On the basis of this consideration, the following fundamental question will be examined as to which normative status can be ascribed to the action of ethical investing itself. Is ethical investing a moral duty of the investor, a benevolent act of solidarity or – to put it provocatively – merely a nice gesture?

At this point, the discussion is again detached from the analysis of the FHG. However, the following thoughts can build on the previous considerations.

3.4 The normative status of the private investor's investment activity

Morally speaking, it is not necessary to invest at all, though if one does invest, it is possible to violate moral claims. Therefore, in order to classify the normative status of an investment activity analytically, a distinction must always be made between the moral assessment of investing as an activity by the investor and the moral assessment of the activities of the objects of investment.[141]

---

141 Cf. Schaefers (2013) 29 and 115.

In ethical investing, it is assumed by definition that there is a causal relationship between these two elements. Depending on the purpose and form of the investor's investment action, the normative status of the investment may vary. This fundamental connection will first be clarified by means of a distinction between speculation and investment. Although speculative investment is not the focus of the present study, it can be used to prepare the ground for discussing the normative status of ethical investing and to further refine the term "ethical investing."

3.4.1 Differences in the normative status of speculation and investment

Speculative investments[142] aim to realise short-term profit by exploiting price differences while simultaneously taking the risk of misjudging price developments into account. In the literature, the moral evaluation of speculation is usually not made dependent on the investor's attitude, but on the consequences of speculation as such. The economic or social benefit or harm to those affected by speculation forms the basis for the assessment.[143] In ethics, the act of speculation is generally regarded as morally legitimate if its consequences do not harm other people.[144] The normative status of speculation itself can initially be described as morally indifferent, i.e., speculation as such is neither morally good nor morally bad, neither necessary nor forbidden. This normative status can also be described as morally permissible (KANT) or morally neutral.[145]

In their normative status, however, specific dimensions of speculation can also be seen as negative duties. A negative duty requires the omission of an action or prohibits a certain action.[146] From an ethical point of view, speculations should be rejected and refrained from if they fulfil certain criteria, for example

142 Graham (2007) 33 gives a classic definition of speculation in contrast to investment. "A capital investment is present if it promises after thorough analysis the security of the assigned capital and a reasonable profit. Investments that do not meet these criteria are considered speculative." Translated by the author [MS].

143 Cf. von Nell-Breuning (1928), 129 ff; Gabriel (2009) 229 f; Schaefers (2013) 117 f.

144 Cf. Gabriel (2009), 230.

145 Cf. Schaefers (2013) 29.

146 Cf. Mieth (2012) 96.

if their risk is no longer limited to the person or institution acting, but if other people suffer damage through speculation and risks are transferred to the general public, e.g., if it destabilises the financial system.[147]

In contrast to speculative investments, an investment is characterised by the fact that in the medium to long term it aims to achieve sustainable capital gains (interest, dividends) from an object of investment. Ethical investing refers to that particular form of investment activity in which a causal relationship between the investment activity and the use of funds is assumed and in which the activities of the object of investment are assessed morally. Determining the normative status of ethical investing as such therefore takes some effort.

Though the act of investing may initially appear to be a morally neutral action, the assumed causality between the investment and the use of funds makes it appear either morally compliant or morally unacceptable.[148] Can one now conclude that the investor in fact does have a moral obligation to invest according to ethical criteria? Is it morally justified to demand that the investor weighs up ethical criteria of the investment (i.e., the use of funds by the object of investment) against his own financial criteria and, if necessary, prioritises ethical criteria?

As the answer to this question may vary depending on the ethical theory and the situation-specific characteristics of the investment (e.g., size, influence on the use of funds), multiple perspectives must be considered.

3.4.2 Ethical investing as an imperfect duty and as a charitable duty

Ethical investing initially appears to be a special kind of imperfect duty in KANT's sense.[149] In contrast to perfect duties, imperfect duties are far-reaching and not strict in their binding force, with their fulfilment being meritorious and not unconditional.[150]

---

147 Cf. Gabriel (2009) 233 f. On the ethical assessment of speculation and the associated risks, cf. also Heinemann (2017) 409 ff and Seiler Zimmermann et al. (2017) 431 ff.

148 Cf. Schaefers (2013) 107 and 132–134.

149 Cf. Ott (1997) 218.

150 Cf. Mieth (2012) 73–75 with reference to Kant's foundation of the metaphysics of morals and Kersting's criticism of Kant's differentiation between perfect and

Imperfect duties are not countered by the rights of others (e.g., rights to freedom or entitlement), which would make them enforceable. The prototype for imperfect duties is the charitable duty. According to BIRNBACHER, the charitable duty requires that every person devote part of his income or time to charitable causes, depending on his or her ability. However, imperfect duties in general and charitable duties in particular are underdetermined. They are not specifically owed to anyone and the obligor has a great deal of discretion in the implementation of these duties. The imperfect duty does not indicate to whom, in what way and when it is to be fulfilled, but merely sets a normative framework. How this normative framework is to be fulfilled is left up to the actor and his non-moral preferences.[151]

The characteristics of ethical investing seem to coincide well with these characteristics of the imperfect charitable duty. It is hardly possible to formulate a strict requirement for ethical investment for the investor. Concerning those possibly affected by negative externalities from the actions of companies, no right to make demands from the investor exists[152] and the investor has a lot of leeway as to how he can invest his assets. Despite this vagueness and a lack of rigour, investors appear to be encouraged to invest ethically, though to be in keeping with moral intuition at the same time. Such a demand seems to have a stronger normative component than to state it simply as admirable to participate, though simultaneously not condemned if refrained from.[153]

Here, the dividing line of a moral-philosophical categorisation of ethical investing runs along a fine line between positive duties (obligations to act) on the one hand and supererogatory acts (acts going beyond the obligatory) on the other. A debate on the allocation to one of these two categories has to deal with different objections. If one argues for the submission of ethical

imperfect duties. Kersting (1997) 76, on the other hand, refers in his critique to that of W.D. Ross to Kant. An approach of conditional duties by Ross is the basis of Chapter 4 of the present study. This approach could be appropriate to address any difficulties with the concept of imperfect obligations via the concept of conditional obligation.

151 Cf. Birnbacher (2013) 131.

152 The underlying problem of justice has already been addressed in Chapter 2 of this study.

153 Cf. Ott (1997) 218.

investing under a broad concept of duty and describes ethical investing as a positive duty, then the question of the strength of this duty and also the question of how to deal with a potential overstretch of the moral capacity of the investor immediately arises.

If, on the other hand, one argues with a rather narrow concept of duty and assigns ethical investing to the category of supererogatory acts, then the problem of overstretching the investor's moral capacity does not arise. However, the question of the binding nature of the normative claim on an investor is all the more difficult to answer, since ethical investing in this case refers to a voluntary effort beyond an obligation.[154] Both categories will be further examined below.

3.4.3 Ethical investing as a weak positive obligation

The concept of positive duty is not clearly defined in the literature and its existence independent of prior behaviour, i.e., its existence independent of prior acts of obligation by an actor,[155] is partly disputed. In line with Birnbacher and Mieth, here, positive (moral) obligations are understood as positive normative rules, which require active effort by the actor, aimed at improving the situation of another person.[156] Positive obligations require a certain action to be taken for moral reasons, as opposed to negative duties that require actions to be refrained from for moral reasons. An example of a positive obligation is the duty to help a person in need, an example of a negative duty is the morally justified prohibition to hurt someone.[157]

The above-mentioned charitable duty therefore falls under the concept of a positive obligation. The concept of a positive duty is also introduced here in order to examine whether a duty to ethical investing is at best stronger than the charitable duty, which has already been recognised as a weak duty.

---

154 Cf. also Mieth (2012) 12. "While the fulfilment of duties can and must be demanded of everyone, this is not the case with supererogatory acts." Translated by the author [MS].

155 For example, contract or family relationship.

156 Cf. Birnbacher (1995) 252; Mieth (2012) 62 f and 11.

157 Cf. Schaefers (2013) 28.

Positive duties are often perceived as weak duties and simultaneously described as choices of action.[158] This distinguishes them from negative duties, which are usually considered strong duties. In the context of investment, negative duties – negative normative rules – apply, for example, to selected areas of speculation, as already shown.

The reason for the frequent assignment of positive duties to weak duties and negative duties to strong duties ultimately lies in the danger of overstretching the moral capacity of actors through positive duties. BIRNBACHER notes that in the case of positive normative rules, the importance of adhering to them is not significant enough to outweigh the costs associated with the moral subjects. He explains.

> "According to this view, positive normative rules have a benefit-cost balance that is less favourable in two respects than negative normative rules: They have a much lower protective effect than negative normative rules, but at the same time they place much higher demands on individual moral resources. Although they are less important to society, they tend to overburden the actors."[159]

In her analysis of positive duties, CORINNA MIETH shows that, contrary to the opinion referred to here, the positive normative rules do not necessarily have to be weak. She therefore proposes differentiating between strong and weak duties even in the case of positive duties and recommends assessing the strength of a rule of action on the basis of the following five criteria.

(1) Needs of the persons concerned,
(2) responsibility of the actor,
(3) reasonableness for the actor,
(4) prospect of success of the action and, if applicable,
(5) admissibility of the action.[160]

MIETH uses these criteria to assess emergency aid obligations in the context of the world poverty problem. In this context of investigating unfair structures, the need of those affected is largely undisputed, as is

158 Cf. Birnbacher (1995) 253.
159 Birnbacher (1995) 253 f, translated by the author [MS].
160 Cf. Mieth (2012) 50 and 168 ff.

the admissibility of assistance provided by persons in affluent countries. However, the criteria of the responsibility of the actors and the prospect of success make it difficult to justify a strong obligation. In this case, the question of the reasonableness for the actor is controversially discussed.

Obviously, the question of the strength of any obligation to ethical investing for a private investor is structurally very different from the question of the assumption of obligations to justice in the context of the world poverty problem. In both cases, the core of the problem lies in the questions of distributive justice and the fairness of institutions. However, the causes, critical variables and solutions of both topics are different from each other.

Despite these fundamental differences between the two topics, it seems appropriate to transfer MIETH's criteria to our problem in order to better define the degree of commitment of a possible obligation to ethical investing.

(1) It is difficult to analytically define the *need for those affected* by ethical investing. This statement applies both to the group of people and moral goods concerned. The group of people affected is ultimately the stakeholder groups of the company which is being invested in. These stakeholder groups can be very heterogeneous (e.g., employees, states, suppliers) and can be distributed across different countries with different legal and cultural standards in the case of internationally active companies. Normative collections of criteria, such as the FHG, can help to determine the moral goods affected by these stakeholder groups. However, unless fundamental moral goods of these stakeholder groups (e.g., human life, health, human rights) are violated in individual cases, from the investor's point of view the nature of the need of those affected can best be understood as the "happiness of others" promoted by ethical investing. Though there will be cases of violations of fundamental human rights by companies, for the majority of cases, this strong criterion of a threat to life, human rights, etc. cannot be postulated without further justification. In most cases, therefore, the criterion of need appears to be fulfilled too little to advocate for a positive obligation to ethical investing.

(2) A certain *responsibility of the investor* in his role as a shareholder and co-owner of a company can, however, be plausibly argued for, even if the concrete extent of this responsibility depends on the individual case

(e.g., degree of directness of the commitment and size of the investment). The fact that an investor, as a co-owner of a company, has a certain degree of responsibility applies even if he is not the sole owner of a company. The fact that the anonymity of the financial markets conceals the visibility and accountability of its jurisdiction does not diminish this argument – at least in theory.

(3) A certain degree of *reasonableness* of investing according to ethical criteria may be assumed with regard to the investor. In individual cases, the reasonableness would have to be measured by the personal and social situation of the investor and also by the potentially lower return of an ethical investment compared to a conventional investment. This raises the central and tricky question of how to draw boundaries. Should it be possible, for example, to demand that all assets be invested according to ethical criteria? Or should one define and justify thresholds for ethical investments that are added to assets invested according to conventional criteria? To what extent would a possible lower return, if any, be acceptable?

(4) The *success of ethical investing* in the form of a positive effect on the moral conduct of individual companies or entire industries can be checked and measured. Although in the case of small investment amounts, a positive effect is only achieved by the sum of many investments, this does not diminish the fundamental validity of the prospect of success in obtaining moral goods by the improved use of funds by companies.

(5) The *admissibility* of the action of ethical investing only seems necessary in regard to the investor, but not in regard to the objects of investment or any other parties concerned. Admissibility may be assumed regarding the parties concerned. On the investor side, however, it is necessary to examine the interests of other people whose rights are potentially diminished by a possible financial loss through an ethical investment (e.g., spouses, children, business partners of the investor).

The preceding line of argumentation roughly outlines how the strength of a positive obligation to ethical investment could be narrowed down in individual cases. It is difficult at this point to make a general judgement that abstracts from the concrete individual case. If all five criteria are considered together, a mixed picture emerges. The obligation to invest ethically still tends to appear weak and with a degree of commitment close to the charitable duty. In a relative comparison with the charitable duty, however, it appears stronger, at least to the extent that the investor's greater responsibility is affirmed. If one also asserts the prospect of success, then judging the need with the criteria of reasonableness and admissibility for the investor and his social environment would become clearer.

Following MIETH, the line between a duty and a supererogatory act can be determined in particular on the basis of the two important criteria of the objective need of the persons concerned and the reasonableness for the actor. If one refers the concept of need of goods such as life and freedom, physical integrity, and other necessary basic goods – food, clothing, shelter, basic medical care[161] – this criterion may not be sufficiently fulfilled in ethical investing in many cases. At the very least, no clear statement can be made as to whether the use of funds by a company in accordance with ethical criteria promotes precisely these – or possibly other – moral goods that provide more "happiness for others".

The examination of ethical investing against the above five criteria thus suggests for the time being that a sense of obligation stronger than the mere duty to be charitable can be established. Due to the difficulty of clearly affirming the criterion of need from the investor's perspective and thus for the use of funds, however, the problem of overstretching the investor's moral capacity still exists.

Can we thus conclude from this that ethical investing should not be regarded as a duty in the strict sense, but rather as a supererogatory act?

3.4.4 Ethical investing as a supererogatory act

The term supererogation refers to an action which reaches beyond duty. First, the actor does more than can be legally or morally demanded of him and second, his action can be judged as morally good.[162] Supererogatory acts go beyond the moral obligation and, at the same time, can run against the inclinations and interests of the actor.[163]

---

161 Cf. Mieth (2012) 45 f.

162 Cf. Urmson (2012) 365 (page number according to the more recent translation of the original English text from 1958); Mieth (2012) 22 f.

163 Cf. Urmson (2012) 381–384.

The concept of supererogation was coined by JAMES URMSON to differentiate between mandatory duties on the one hand, and morally good, but not obligatory actions on the other hand. In his work entitled "Saints and Heroes" URMSON calls for the following.

> "A line must be drawn between what we can expect and demand from others and what we can merely hope for and receive with gratitude when we get it; duty falls on one side of this line, and other acts with moral value on the other, and rightly so."[164]

URMSON thus assumes a *narrow concept of duty* and pleads to reserve it for an absolutely compelling minimal moral in explaining.

> "It is a part of the notion of Duty in every one of its forms, that a person may rightfully be compelled to fulfil it. Duty is a thing which may be exacted from a person, as one exacts a debt. Unless we think that it may be exacted from him, we do not call it his duty. ... There are other things, on the contrary, which we wish that people should do, which we like or admire them for doing, perhaps dislike or despise them for not doing, but yet admit that they are not bound to do; it is not a case of moral obligation; we do not blame them, that is, we do not think that they are proper objects of punishment."[165]

Although supererogatory acts do not fall under a narrow compulsory concept and are therefore not morally binding, URMSON postulates that a supererogatory act can nevertheless be compelling from the point of view of the actor, in order to correspond to the ideals of the actor.[166]

In ethics, two types of supererogation are distinguished according to the degree of reasonableness of an action. First, an unreasonable degree of fulfilling duties as it is expressed in the actions of "Saints and Heroes". This understanding corresponds to URMSON's classical definition. Second, a reasonable level of performing obligations. This understanding corresponds to CORINNA MIETH's interpretation of the term and describes an action whose execution we praise but whose omission we do not denounce, e.g., donations for the hungry.[167]

164 Urmson (1958) 213.
165 Urmson (1953) 36.
166 Cf. Urmson (2012) 382–384.
167 Cf. Horster (2012) 61.

The second understanding of the concept of supererogation forms the basis of the following discussion. It is devoted to the question of whether ethical investing is a supererogatory act of the investor that is morally good but not obligatory, and that the actor carries out in order to stay aligned with his moral ideals.

The preceding question is occasionally affirmed in the literature. According to OTT, ethical investing undeniably has elements of a supererogatory act, even though a categorical classification is not entirely clear from his point of view.[168] The subcategory of ethical investments in the form of sustainable investments at least, is clearly described as a supererogatory act by SCHAEFERS. He argues that, in this case, investors perform morally good but not morally binding actions that deserve moral recognition because they are selflessly motivated.[169]

For ethical investments in general, however, SCHAEFERS distinguishes between their moral and ideational dimensions. He assigns supererogatory acts to the ideational dimension of ethical investing, i.e., to the orientation towards ideals which, although rooted in morality, are not characterised by an obligation.[170] In contrast to the ideational dimension of ethical investments, their moral dimension should be narrower. SCHAEFERS specifies the moral dimension of investments as follows.

> "Investments are, among other things, morally compliant if the actions of the objects of investment corresponding to them ... at least do not damage the conditions for satisfying the justified fundamental basic needs of future generations, but instead help to preserve them. ... Investments are ... then morally consistent, if the objects of the moral evaluation ... respect the fundamental rights of life, health, and subsistence level for the future generations. ... For example, a stock investment is morally unacceptable if, among other things, it acts irresponsibly in the long term, i.e., if the actions of the invested companies disregard the basic moral rights of future generations, for example by discharging environmentally harmful waste water into rivers during the production process or by contaminating soil with chemicals."[171]

168 Cf. Ott (1997) 219.
169 Cf. Schaefers (2013) 34.
170 Cf. Schaefers (2013) 30–32.
171 Schaefers (2013) 206 (partly italic in the original), translated by the author [MS].

In the context of a sustainability discussion, SCHAEFERS' definition emphasises the cross-generational dimensions of ethical investing. Yet, it seems legitimate to relate the moral needs addressed to present generations as well. The definition is far from exhaustive and can be extended in several respects.

However, the following observation appears more important than a discussion of possible additional dimensions at this point. SCHAEFERS' distinction between moral and ideational dimensions of ethical investing ultimately leads to the realisation that the concept of ethical investing itself is too broad to be clearly assigned a normative status.

Assuming a broad definition of ethical investing, as in the practice of the financial services industry, the literature, and the present study, ethical investing reveals elements of a charitable duty, a weak positive duty, or a supererogatory act.

If, on the other hand, the concept of ethical investing is defined very narrowly and if, for example, it is strictly related to the (indirect) participation of an investor in harming fundamental rights of persons affected by the objects of investment, then an obligation for ethical investing could possibly be postulated. Due to its binding nature, the obligation for ethical investing could be much stronger than is expressed by the charitable duty or by a supererogatory act.

In view of the foregoing considerations, it seems important at this point to note three observations as a brief interim conclusion.

(1) It is initially difficult to classify the normative status of ethical investing because the concept of ethical investing itself is too broad to be able to assign it clearly. The narrower the term is defined, for example, by exclusively including the violation of human rights by the objects of investment, the more stringent are any obligations for the investor which can be derived from it. Methodologically, one would probably, in this case, tend to postulate negative obligations of the investor rather than positive obligations, for example, that an investor should exclude certain investments in principle. Ethical investing would then be reduced by definition to limiting an investor's investment universe according to strict moral criteria. In fact, this approach would amount to a negative selection of objects of investment, similar to what we

have already seen in the behaviour of the historical precursors of ethical investing.

(2) If, on the other hand, the concept of ethical investing is broadly defined, as is the case in the present study and generally also in theory and practice, then it is more difficult to give moral reasons for any obligation to invest ethically. Ethical investing then appears more like a charitable duty or a supererogatory act. In both cases, which are, by the way, very close to each other in terms of content, the investor would subjectively justify the demand for ethical investing. He would be aligning himself towards his own moral ideals.[172]

(3) In her analysis of positive duties, MIETH points out that the determination of duties can change depending on institutional and epistemic conditions.[173] Considering this assumption, the idea could be put up for discussion that institutional and epistemic frameworks in ethical investing have recently moved in a direction that are suitable to either stringently establish a duty to ethical investing in the future or – if such a duty is already assumed – to possibly strengthen it. A wide range of financial intermediaries and investment vehicles are currently emerging institutionally, offering an increasingly broad public the opportunity to invest ethically. This trend goes hand in hand with a growing level of transparency and greater knowledge of the interrelationships of ethical investment thanks to new technologies. These developments strengthen the sensitivity of investors and at the same time increase the objective as well as the subjective pressure on investors to be able to justify their own investments according to moral criteria. Changing institutional and epistemic frameworks should therefore make it easier to strengthen a positive obligation to ethical investment in the future.

3.5 Interim conclusion

The explanations above have touched on different theoretical positions and have also looked at different areas of the subject. The opportunities and challenges of morally justified investing can only be assessed meaningfully

172 Schaefers' argumentation (2013) 162 aims in this direction.
173 Cf. Mieth (2012) 241.

with regard to a clearly defined area of subject matter and against the background of a selected ethical theory. Consequently, the opportunities and challenges of ethical investing must be viewed in a differentiated way against the background of the foregoing.

The preference-utilitarian approach to assessing the moral conduct of companies is strongly connected to economic reason[174] and is very effective in mediating between pluralistic value systems. These fundamental strengths of preference utilitarianism may have contributed to the fact that the FHG, which builds on this ethical theory, enjoys a high degree of acceptance in the practice of the financial services industry. It has a formative influence on "best-in-class" concepts of the stock selection of ethical funds. Ethical investments of billions of assets are based on this approach, which can be seen as a great strength of this approach.

Nevertheless, an important challenge posed to this approach is the fact that it cannot ultimately justify the binding nature of even basic norms – such as human rights – and demand binding force from companies. Even the recourse to fundamental moral rules such as those defined by BERNHARD GERT cannot defuse this problem. An investor who orients him- or herself to the theory and method of the FHG is not capable of resolving either inner-ethical conflicts or conflicts between moral and financial criteria. Ultimately, he or she will experience difficulties in orientation. In such a situation a normative framework comprising principles with subordinating power is required.[175]

Since preference utilitarianism cannot establish any binding moral obligations for companies, it cannot contribute to establishing such an obligation for the action of ethical investment itself, since it is by definition dependent on it.

When regarding the investment activity itself as an object, a deontological (obligatory) ethics, e.g., of the Kantian type, is able to justify supreme compulsory principles and demand their unconditional validity. If these

---

174 For the concept of economic reason cf. Thurnherr (2001) 134–136; Thurnherr (2010) 94 ff.

175 Cf. Werner (2011a) 17 on the criticism of the lack of subordination in the rules put forward by Gert.

duties are perfect duties, then they are generally able to subordinate.[176] In our concrete case of application, however, this approach reaches its limit in terms of content as it is difficult to classify ethical investing as a perfect duty. The investment activity appears to be a special case of an imperfect duty with its element of obligation thus tending to be weak. The normative status of ethical investing is categorically close to a charitable duty or a supererogatory act. This applies even in the case where a more pronounced morally binding component is affirmed due to the responsibility of a shareholder in the corporate action of the objects of investment. The postulate of a strong obligation to ethical investing is likely to fail even simply due to the linguistic expanse and vagueness of the term "ethical investing".

Therefore in our case, even different forms of a deontological approach cannot easily solve the challenge of weighing up conflicting norms against each other. As a solution, two approaches seem reasonable. Either one defines the term "ethical investing" very narrowly, refers it exclusively to fundamental rights that may be violated by a company's actions, and from this, derives negative investment obligations for the investor. This would in fact require a (strong) obligation for a negative selection of investments. Alternatively, one can look for ways in which the issue of weighing up conflicting norms can be solved methodically. This approach will be examined in more detail in the following chapter.

176 Cf. Werner (2011a) 17.

4 Considerations by the investor

In Chapter 2, the interdependencies between the investment activity of a private investor on the one hand and the activity of companies as targets of investment on the other, were shown. The argument was put forward that an investor as a shareholder and thus co-owner of a company also bears a moral responsibility for its actions, which he can and *should* fulfil. Finally, the criteria for weighing up the moral and financial criteria of the investment were sought.

Chapter 3 presented a comprehensive collection of criteria for the moral evaluation of companies. First, the opportunities and challenges in the justification and application of the moral evaluation of the actions of companies were examined. In a second step, the normative status of ethical investing as an investment activity in itself was discussed. In this discussion, questions of weighing up moral and financial aspects of the investment played a role again, but they were not yet set as the focus of the investigation.

The discussion so far has shown that a well-founded collection of criteria for the selection of objects of investment is central to the process of ethical investing. First, to guide an investor's reflected actions and, second, to be able to analyse and reflect on the normative status of ethical investing.

At the same time, it became apparent that a collection of criteria for ethical investing is not simply a recipe book that an investor must faithfully apply in practice. A collection of criteria is always based on its own theory and requires weighing up and evaluating criteria in the application. In practice, it is therefore necessary for the investor to reflect on his own set of criteria and, based on this, to autonomously carry out additional *steps of mediation* in order to apply ethical investing.

An investor's overall assessment of an investment then requires not only a prudent analysis of the situation of the object of investment and one's own starting point, but also to weigh all of the morally justified and financial aspects. In this case, moral criteria for assessing the use of funds can provide orientation and guidance. The concrete application of the investor, however, requires weighing up moral and financial criteria, which often conflict with each other in practice.

But according to which principles can it be justified for the investor to weigh criteria up against each other?

4.1 Weighing up criteria on the basis of prima facie duties

The idea of weighing up criteria means that a decision in a situation of conflicting norms must be based on objective aspects, but that there is no formalised procedure and no imperative rule that generally indicates an order of priority between the aspects.[177] RICKEN formulates the question of choosing the right alternative.

> "The right decision can therefore only be found with the help of practical judgement, which weighs up these different aspects against each other. In many cases there will be room for discretion. Even simply based on different experiences, aspects can be weighed up differently. A person acts responsibly when she makes every effort, within the limits of her possibilities, to find the relevant aspects for a decision and when she is able and willing to explain how and for what reasons she personally weights within the framework of these objective conditions. ... Practical judgement requires experience and practice. The practical truth is a regulative idea that an individual practical judgement seeks to approximate."[178]

In search for the right alternative for action, the investor will orientate himself implicitly or explicitly by superordinate rules in an applied decision-making situation in which conflicts of norms cannot be resolved. These meta rules themselves can be normative principles or middle-level rules that mediate between the level of basic ethical norms and the level of concrete options for action. These are considered plausible when the opposing rule cannot be seriously considered. Middle-level principles and rules often have a certain plausibility, but they have to be specified to a certain situation. In addition, they must demonstrate their relevance in order to develop their argumentative power within the framework of a practical chain of argumentation.[179]

Within the framework of conventional investments, there are numerous rules that offer orientation in dealing with conflicts of interest in traditional investments. GRAHAM OR KLARMANN, for example, propose the rule of

177 Cf. Ricken (2003) 224.
178 Ricken (2003) 224, translated by the author [MS].
179 Cf. Bobbert (2012) 390 f.

adhering to a margin of safety to control the return and risk of an investment.[180] To the best of the author's knowledge [MS], however, so far there are few or even no middle-level rules that are relevant and plausible for investment decisions in the areas of normative conflict in ethical investing that include moral criteria in their considerations.[181]

In this situation, two approaches appear to go further by creating a basis for such rules in the field of ethical investing. However, it should be noted that such an initial proposal must remain provisional in the context of this investigation. The two following approaches and rules are intended as proposals that appear promising but can and must be further differentiated scientifically and practically with regard to ethical investing.

First, the pluralistic deontological approach from DAVID ROSS,[182] second the principles of applied ethics from the authors GABRIEL/SCHLAGNITWEIT.[183] Both approaches have a certain similarity in their logic and could thus complement each other.

ROSS's approach is a far-reaching, theoretically sound ethical approach, but it does not relate to the concrete practice of ethical investing. It is chosen here because it contains theoretical elements, the combination of which seems to be of further relevance for our particular type of question (deontology, teleology and virtue ethics).

GABRIEL/SCHLAGNITWEIT's approach does not reveal its ethical background theory in detail, but refers directly to the practice of ethical investing of private investors. For this reason, it appears adequate for this discussion.

Thus, the suggestion put forward here is that each of these two approaches can be considered as continuations of the search for balancing considerations in ethical investing. In addition, the thesis is put forward that these two approaches could possibly complement each other in order to develop a basis for middle-level principles of ethical investing. The two

180 Cf. primarily Graham (2007) and Klarman (1991); also Pardoe (2005).

181 For rules on the weighing of goods and quantitative preferential rules of general ethics, cf. Ricken (2003) 243–248. Bobbert (2012) 391–395 gives an overview of middle-level rules in the context of application using the example of medical ethics. Scholand (2004) 156–165 contains heuristics of judgements on the reduction of complexity and quick decisions in the investment sector.

182 Cf. Ross (1976) 253–269; Horster (2009) 34–37.

183 Cf. Gabriel/Schlagnitweit (2009) 73–80.

approaches are juxtaposed and interpreted with a view to their application. In terms of content, however, the two approaches are deliberately not mixed because of their different areas of origin and subject matter, as well as their different scope. Such an approach of drafting middle-level principles of ethical investing must remain provisional in the context of this study, but it may provide starting points for further studies.

In a decision-making situation marked by conflicts of norms, Ross postulates the observance of so-called "prima facie duties", which he also calls "conditional duties".[184] Although, due to a lack of better terminology, these are referred to as duties, they are not actual duties, but principles of evaluation, with their concrete constellation deciding how an actor is obliged to balance normative rules. The evaluation principles are thus intended as a starting point for a rational consideration of the morally significant aspects of an action.[185]

Ross essentially distinguishes six or seven prima facie duties, or ways everyone ought to act, which provide guidance as assessment principles. He does not claim this list is exhaustive or final.

(1) *Duties depending on previous acts.*
 a. *Duty of fidelity.* Promise keeping.
 b. *Duty of reparation.* Making up for prior wrongful acts.
(2) *Duty of gratitude.* Being grateful for others' acts of kindness.
(3) *Duty of justice.* Being fair.
(4) *Duty of beneficence.* Benefiting or helping others.
(5) *Duty of self-improvement.* Education or practice.
(6) *Duty of non-maleficence.* Not harming others.[186]

The prima facie duty of non-maleficence is a subcategory of the duty of benefice. It is the only duty to be formulated negatively and it is deliberately stated separately because of the higher degree of urgency and commitment it demands.[187]

184 Cf. Ross (1976) 256; Birnbacher (2013) 160 f; Birnbacher/Hoerster (1976) 235.
185 Cf. Birnbacher (2013) 161 and 437.
186 Cf. Ross (1930) 21 f.
187 Cf. Ross (1976) 257 f.

From the author's [MS] point of view, the prima facie duties can serve to support the argumentation of an investor in decision-making situations in order to be able to rationally justify moral judgements. The advantage they offer is their determination in terms of content and materiality. However, this must be further specified for the concrete situation. From the collection of conditional duties mentioned above, the *duty of non-maleficence,* the *duty of justice*, the *duty of beneficence* and the *duty of self-improvement,* in particular, appear to be meaningful assessment principles for weighing up moral and financial norms in a situation with conflicting goals. The *duty of reparation* and the *duty of gratitude,* on the other hand, do not appear to be directly relevant in the context of ethical investing.

Prima facie duties must be interpreted by the ethical investor. How such an interpretation can be made in the context of financial investment is illustrated with the following example, without claiming to be exhaustive.

(1) *Duty of non-maleficence.* This prima facie duty can be interpreted as a guideline to establish clear *exclusion criteria* for investments. For an investor, this should cover those companies that are highly likely to harm other people, e.g., by violating human rights or damaging the health of human life and/or the environment. An investor should be able to provide a strong rationale should he violate this prima facie obligation for financial benefits.

(2) *Duty of justice.* This prima facie duty refers primarily to the *justice of the distribution* of pleasure or happiness or the means to it. It aims to eliminate or prevent a distribution that has been recognised as unfair.[188] In the context of ethical investing, the duty of justice can be seen, for example, in the fact that the inequality of material rights between the production factors of capital on the one hand, and labour or nature on the other is to be recognised and at least partially eliminated by the investor. An investor can fulfil this duty of justice by waiving part of the return on capital of his or her investment in order to privilege the production factors of labour or nature, e.g., through a *positive selection* of morally eligible investments.

188 Cf. Ross (1976) 257.

(3) *Duty of beneficence.* In the context of ethical investing, this prima facie duty can be used as a reminder of the requirement that an investor should not only base his or her investment on his or her own financial criteria, but should also take others into account in every investment and, if possible, improve their situation through an investment.

(4) *Duty of self-improvement.* This prima facie duty focuses on the "subjective" aspect of an investment activity. It can, for example, be interpreted as meaning that it is necessary for an actor to expand his investment competence not only financially but also morally.

According to Ross, the decision as to which mandatory principle should be decisive in a decision-making situation is left to the individual assessment of the situation (limited by the relative urgency of the duty of non-maleficence).[189] In this respect, Ross's approach does not ultimately provide any clear guidance on how to assign weight to moral and financial criteria when they conflict in concrete situations. However, with a manageable number of evaluation principles, this deontological approach provides bridging elements that can facilitate practical reasoning by mediating between ethical theory and empirical application. Observing prima facie duties can help clarify the rationale of a chosen investment in the process of creating a balance between moral and financial goals.

In addition, Ross emphasises the important task of obtaining a solid overview of the situation as a first step, in the event of conflicting standards. Ross identifies this task as the true duty of the actor.

> "When I am in a situation, as perhaps I always am, in which more than one of these *prima facie* duties is incumbent on me, what I have to do is to study the situation as fully as I can until I form the considered opinion (it is never more) that in the circumstances one of them is more incumbent than any other; then I am bound to think that to do this *prima facie* duty is my duty *sans phrase* in the situation."[190]

---

189 Cf. Birnbacher/Hoerster (1976) 234.

190 Ross (1930) 19 emphasis in original.

4.2 Middle-level principles to support orientation in situations of conflict

Similar to Ross, the authors Gabriel and Schlagnitweit also address the question of how to deal with moral grey areas and ethical conflicts of interest in application. Unlike Ross, however, Gabriel/Schlagnitweit's considerations relate directly to the practice of ethical investing. They assume the following.

> "... that ethics that is suitable and relevant for everyday use can by no means be limited to formulating noble moral imperatives without keeping their actual feasibility in mind. Rather, it must provide normative support for concrete and often unavoidable decision-making situations."[191]

Gabriel/Schlagnitweit formulate four basic principles by which an ethically oriented investor should align herself in moral borderland.[192]

(1) Principle of moral obligation dependent on personal capability.
(2) Principle of minimizing harm by choosing the lesser evil.
(3) Principle of weighing up goods against each other based on a justified hierarchy of values.
(4) Principle of pragmatic, iterative development of the competence in ethical investing.[193]

To some extent, these four basic principles overlap with Ross's assessment principles, but they are not the same. For example, the principle of minimizing harm according to Gabriel/Schlagnitweit[194] is close to Ross's prima facie duty of non-maleficence. The principle described by Ross as a duty to self-improvement finds a certain correspondence in Principles 1 and 4 of Gabriel/Schlagnitweit, which refer to the personal competence of the investor.

---

191 Gabriel/Schlagnitweit (2009) 74 f, translated by the author [MS].

192 Cf. Gabriel/Schlagnitweit (2009) 75–79, formulation of the four principles slightly adapted by the author [MS] to improve readability and comprehensibility.

193 Gabriel/Schlagnitweit summarise this principle under the title "pragmatic-dynamic ethics." Cf. Gabriel/Schlagnitweit (2009) 78.

194 Cf. Gabriel/Schlagnitweit (2009) 76.

Gabriel/Schlagnitweit's principles, like the prima facie duties laid down by Ross, thus both refer to "objective" aspects of a decision-making situation (principles 2 and 3) and to "subjective" aspects, which look into the possibilities an actor has (principles 1 and 4). The judgement of reason has to capture objective and subjective aspects equally. How these principles can be interpreted in detail in the context of their application is described below.

4.2.1 Personal capability both limits and expands moral duties

The principle of "moral obligation dependent on personal capability" initially serves to protect against overstretching the moral capacity of the investor and refers to the traditional moral principle "Ultra posse nemo tenetur" ["No one is obligated beyond what he or she is able to do"]. According to this principle, a moral duty is restrained by the competence and possibilities of the actor. Among the possibilities of the actor are, for example, his mental and physical abilities, education, social relations, possessions, and financial possibilities. The possibilities of the actor either restrict the idea of what should be done or they expand it. This aspect, according to which capability is always a prerequisite for being able to achieve what should be done, must be taken into account in the reasoning of decision making.[195]

Gabriel/Schlagnitweit interpret the principle of the "ultra posse nemo tenetur" in the context of ethical investing primarily as meaning that *no one can be morally obliged beyond her personal capability*. They explain.

> "Where a person (despite a conscientious search for it) actually has no (reasonable) alternatives to an ethically problematic action, she cannot be held morally accountable. A person can only be held responsible for her actions to the extent that there is room for discretion."[196]

In the context of ethical investing, the reference to the personal capability of the actor can, from the author's point of view [MS], also be understood to have a second connotation that goes beyond the meaning of competence. "Capability" may not only denote the comprehensive personal ability of the

195 Cf. Ricken (2003) 246; Gabriel/Schlagnitweit (2009) 75 f.
196 Gabriel/Schlagnitweit (2009) 75, translated by the author [MS].

investor, but also emphasise the specific aspect of his ability which is determined by the disposable financial assets of the investor.[197] This rule could then not only be understood as a negative protection against overstretching the moral capacity of an investor, as GABRIEL/SCHLAGNITWEIT recommend, but also as a positive duty in the sense of a growing moral obligation depending on the quantitative size of the investable assets.

The amount of disposable financial assets – in absolute quantity as well as relative to the needs of the investor – is an important aspect from the point of view of assessing the consequences of investment decisions in general. With an increasing size of assets, the number of investment options increases as may potentially the degree of direct influence which an investor can exert on the morally consistent use of funds (keywords here are "active shareholder engagement").

At the same time, one could argue that, with growing wealth, it becomes more reasonable to accept possible financial losses for the sake of ethical objectives. The rule can thus be further specified in the sense that with increasing assets, the investment to be selected is the one that fulfils a greater number of moral criteria or the one that grants a higher degree of direct influence on the use of the funds in line with moral criteria.

4.2.2 Minimizing harm by choosing the lesser evil

The rule of minimizing harm requires that in situations of ethical conflict the lesser evil should always be chosen. This balancing rule also focuses on the consequences of an action, though it presupposes a concrete definition of evil as well as of values or goods. The rule of choosing the lesser evil has a long moral-philosophical and theological tradition and is already found in ARISTOTLE and THOMAS AQUINAS. Usually, in the discussion of this rule a distinction is made between moral and physical evils. *Moral evils* include wrong decisions of one's free will against the morally good, *physical evils* include morally indifferent states such as pain, suffering, illness or death, which can be caused by humans or by force majeure.[198]

---

197 Gabriel/Schlagnitweit (2009) do not show any deliberate ambiguity in the talk of "capabilities". They use the term as a synonym for the individual competence of the investor.

198 Cf. Bruch (1981) 166 f; Wolbert (1990) 806 f.

According to GABRIEL/SCHLAGNITWEIT, the rule in the context of ethical investing can be understood as follows.

> "This means two things for the question of investing: a) There is a moral obligation for investors to never solely pay attention to the greatest possible return in their investment decisions, but also to the consequences of their decisions for people, society, and the environment in accordance with all available information possibilities – and to choose from comparable investment alternatives those which have the least negative consequences for these stakeholders. b) Moreover, every person is obliged in her conscience to balance profit entitlements of persons or financial institutions against the possible consequences thereof and, if necessary, to take alternatives, even if these entail a reduction in expected returns.[199]

In practice, it will be necessary to define this rule and its underlying concepts even more precisely in order to be able to justify moral judgements. In order to weigh up the consequences of action against each other, they should also be determined in more detail with regard to their intensity, duration, certainty or uncertainty, proximity or distance, probability of occurrence, severity of a possible risk, and other relevant factors.[200]

4.2.3 Weighing up goods based on a justified hierarchy of values

GABRIEL/SCHLAGNITWEIT interpret the principle of weighing up goods based on a justified hierarchy of values as a call to compromise in the choice between moral values that are not easily harmonised with one another. If it is a challenge to bring moral values into a clear hierarchy when investing, one should not act rigorously and not be discouraged by the complexity of the decision-making situation, but persistently seek compromises with regard to financial and ethical criteria.[201]

The search for compromises should, however, be guided by a clearly understandable hierarchy of moral values, so that decisions can be justified on the basis of reason. GABRIEL/SCHLAGNITWEIT state with reference to the necessary sense of reality in financial investments.

---

199 Gabriel/Schlagnitweit (2009) 76 (partly italic in the original), translated by the author [MS]. Cf. similar to Hanke (1999) 416.

200 Cf. Bobbert (2012) 394 f and Ricken (2003) 248.

201 Cf. Gabriel/Schlagnitweit (2009) 77.

> "Anyone who behaves too rigorously in the area of investment ... and wants all the ethical criteria mentioned to be considered absolutely without compromise can easily find herself in a situation where there are no or at least no realistic investment opportunities on the capital market with regard to the necessary risk, liquidity or return requirements. ... Here it is particularly clear that ethically motivated action must never exclude the relation to reality and in many cases requires the willingness or ability to compromise. The accusation of 'shaky' compromises need not be feared by anyone who can justify her decisions comprehensibly with a formulated hierarchy of values and, accordingly, based on a conscientious process of ethical consideration of the goods."[202]

The rule of weighing goods can also be further enriched and specified in terms of content within an argumentation on ethical investing. This can be done, for example, by giving the necessary moral goods an unconditional priority over less necessary goods in the process of balancing criteria.[203] In such a process of weighing up moral goods, a collection of criteria such as the FHG can provide support in identifying the necessary goods, increasing their priority and weighting them accordingly.

4.2.4 Pragmatic and dynamic learning process to develop investor competence

In practice, private investment is often regarded as an issue of "low interest", which at the same time has a high degree of factual complexity. Due to a lack of interest, private investors often only have limited expertise in investment matters. A complex balancing process between moral and financial investment criteria can therefore be all the more challenging for an investor, since the factual dimension of the investment itself makes it difficult to judge.

In this situation, GABRIEL/SCHLAGNITWEIT recommend a pragmatic and dynamic learning process to build the competence of an ethical investor. Again, this middle-level rule thus refers to a subjective point of view with regard to the possibilities of the investor. In contrast to the first rule, which aims to protect against overstretching the investor's moral capacity, the fourth rule encourages the investor to build up and further develop her own

202 Gabriel/Schlagnitweit (2009) 77, translated by the author [MS].
203 Cf. Bobbert (2012) 391 f; Ricken (2003) 244–246.

ethical competence in investments in a continuous and gradual learning process. Conscious of imprecision, lack of transparency, faulty and insufficient sources of information, the investor should be patient and at the same time persistent in the conscientious process of weighing up ethical goods. GABRIEL/SCHLAGNITWEIT write about this.

> "Such processes can be very tedious, must ... be repeated and renewed over and over again and never give the feeling of certainty that all ethical responsibility requirements have been fulfilled completely, without error or even with regard to reason. ... In a first step, it is better to subject one's investment decisions only to individual, realisable ethical criteria than to none at all – and, with growing ethical competence, a growing information base and perhaps also growing possibilities for action, to gradually and continuously further develop one's originally perhaps still rudimentary ethical criteria."[204]

The rule of building up a competence of ethical investing in a simple, gradual process of learning and on the basis of an independent criteriology appears relevant and plausible in the context of investment in the sense that it corresponds to analogous rules of conventional investment. At a first glance, the following exemplary rules seem to be theoretically trivial. To implement these rules consistently, however, is very demanding in practice.

The first four of WARREN BUFFETT's (purely financial) investment principles are: "Give preference to the simple over the difficult", "Be patient", "Keep a cool head" and "Think for yourself".[205] In his seminal work on stock investment, BENJAMIN GRAHAM recommends that the ideal type of intelligent investor should be trained in the rules of patience, discipline, the desire to learn and also in independent thinking.[206] When making sustainable investments, MISSBACH demands: "The first commandment for dealing responsibly with money is: 'You shall form an opinion for yourself'."[207]

The same might be demanded for the ideal type of an "ethical investor" if he or she makes "mixed" judgements in which financial expertise and moral discernment are seamlessly interconnected.

---

204 Gabriel/Schlagnitweit (2009) 78, translated by the author [MS].
205 Cf. Pardoe (2005) 8, translated by the author [MS].
206 Cf. Graham (2007) 28.
207 Missbach (2007) 48, translated by the author [MS].

4.3 Interim conclusion

Having to balance moral and financial investment criteria against each other represents one of the key challenges for ethical investing. Since a duty to invest ethically can be understood as imperfect and normatively under-determined, a hierarchy of moral norms and values in relation to financial goals – or vice versa – is not necessarily easy to establish in practice. Nevertheless, in order to be able to make a practical judgement, reason needs to be guided by certain rules that have the character of meta rules, i.e., that stand in a superordinate position to the judging criteria.

The prima facie duties put forward by Ross, as well as the middle-level principles by Gabriel/Schlagnitweit could be understood as such meta rules of ethical investing. In the interpretation given here, these two approaches could encourage an investor to place him- or herself in a critical and distanced relationship to the investment activity and its criteria in a first step, and then, in a second step, the investor would aim to arrive at a well-founded practical judgement taking into account all relevant objective as well as subjective aspects. Neither the approach from Ross nor that of Gabriel/Schlagnitweit can normatively resolve issues of balancing. However, both proposals can offer further approaches in terms of content and process.

Ross's pluralistic deontological approach is based on concrete duties that are relevant in order to rationally weigh up the morally significant aspects of action against each other in a concrete situation of application. In contrast to utilitarian ethics, this approach acknowledges, for example, a duty of justice, in particular that of fair distribution.[208] It is precisely this prima facie duty – in addition to the duty of non-maleficence – that should have a central place in the moral justification of investment activities, because ethical investing is essentially based on problems of distributive justice and the fairness of institutions.

The strength of Gabriel/Schlagnitweit's principles lies in their emphasis on the process. These normative principles are intended to guide an investor in how he or she can independently make progress on the path to ethically reflected investment decisions and methodically

208 Cf. Birnbacher/Hoerster (1976) 231.

address moral considerations. He or she could do this, for example, by searching for alternative courses of action, by being comprehensively informed about the consequences of investment decisions, by being prepared to compromise even in areas of normative conflict, and by eventually building up and developing his or her own competence of ethical investing.

In particular, the subjective aspects of ethical investing emphasised by GABRIEL/SCHLAGNITWEIT must consider a discussion of the opportunities and challenges of a morally justified investment. In the person and ethical authority of the investor lies both an opportunity for moral reason of the investment as well as a limit, in the long run: The more competent an investor is both technically and in his ability to ethically judge, the closer he or she will approximate the governing idea of a practical truth in questions of moral consideration. In this sense, ethical investing could not only be understood as an ethically reflected investment activity, but also as a process of individually building up an ethically sound competence in investment issues.

For the reasons given above, the two approaches discussed seem to have the potential to provide individual investors with guidance on the moral considerations of an investment. They are *put up for discussion* in the present study because relevant middle-level rules for the area of ethical investing do not yet exist for the private investor. From a scientific point of view, however, it seems important to point out that a systematic ethical argumentation based on one of these two approaches in order to derive moral judgement in investment transactions requires numerous further steps of mediation.

For example, applying ROSS's prima facie duties to investment issues requires not only further clarification and interpretation of some basic concepts (e.g., justice), but also a more detailed justification of how and why these duties are to be put into concrete effect for an investor.

GABRIEL/SCHLAGNITWEIT's approach would have to be examined in detail regarding its theoretical premises: With reference to an ethical theory, the opportunities and challenges of the principle of weighing goods or of the principle of choosing the lesser evil should be pointed out in particular.

Due to the aim and scope of the present study, these theoretical and practical challenges in dealing with the proposed principles can merely be pointed out.[209] The discussion of these principles could be the subject of further studies on ethical investing.

209 Cf. Streiff (2017) 233–245 for an example of weighing moral criteria in the investment process and the role of an Ethics Committee at the Swiss wealth management firm Hauck & Aufhäuser (Schweiz) AG.

5 Opportunities and challenges of ethical investing

The starting point of the present study was the observation of a trend towards so-called "ethical investing." Ethical investing is a very broad collective term that describes the selection of financial investments not only from a financial point of view, but also according to moral principles. In particular, ethical investing aims to counter a problem of distributive justice between the production factors of capital on the one hand and human labour or nature on the other, by steering capital flows at the micro and meso level: An investor seeks to influence the economic action of the targets of investment by selecting his or her investments, e.g., equity investments in companies, according to whether these targets of investment are consistent with fundamental moral principles, norms, and values in their actions and behaviours.

Against this background, the present study has sought the moral principles based on which a private investor can and *should* make his or her decisions. It has also pointed out various opportunities and challenges of a morally justified investment. The key findings are summarized below.

The historical precursors of ethical investing, for example, the Quakers, Methodists or Sharia-compliant banking, primarily justify their selection of investments with reference to their religious norms and values and to some extent directly refer to the knowledge of revelation such as the New Testament or the Koran. Based on these criteria, they formulate negative criteria. These call on the members of the religious communities to exclude certain investments, for example investments in weapons, addictive substances or human trafficking.

In the twentieth century, ethical investing reached beyond the circle of religious communities and the rationality of moral criteria for investments gained importance. Starting in North America, then followed in the last 10–15 years by German-speaking countries, these investment criteria typically place a triad of economic, social/cultural, and ecological selection criteria at the centre of ethical investing. The observance of fundamental human rights, intragenerational justice between industrialised and developing countries, intergenerational justice between generations, or bio-survival security are defined as goals and standards of ethical investing, which are further validated respectively.

However, the justification of such goals and criteria represents a challenge from the point of view of ethical theory and its practical implementation in the individual actions of private investors *and* companies. This challenge starts with the broad definition of the term "ethical investing" itself.

The broad semantic field of the term "ethical investing" can be seen as an opportunity to sensitise financial market actors for ethical issues. Questions about the moral acceptability of the use of financial means as well as problems of distributive justice and the fairness of institutions can be considered in a broad discourse. In this way, a theoretical and practical contribution can be made to enhance moral standards in the financial services industry, the economy, and society.

The downside and limitation of a broad definition, however, are that the term runs the risk of being used in a meaningless, inflationary and misappropriated way. Financial market players such as fund providers or banks – or even relevant financial advisors – then justify their recommendations on ethical investing with their financial attractiveness and thus miss the core of the topic in their justification. Ethical investments, e.g., in corresponding equity funds, are then presented as a future-oriented topic with a possible financial outperformance. They are justified by a financial return based on moral deliberation. The critical question as to what minimum return would be acceptable for an investor to help implement moral principles by companies is, however, not addressed. In this case, the concept and justification of ethical investment are counterproductive rather than desirable. Instead of promoting transparency in order to advocate for morally appropriate action by economic subjects, it merely appeals to the economic calculus and instrumental reason of investors.

An ethical approach must be based on the obligation that an investment should be made according to moral criteria even if it results in financial disadvantages for the investor. The issue that lies at the core of ethical investing is therefore that of a justified balance between moral and financial investment criteria.

However, a balancing judgement can only be meaningfully postulated if – as in our study – the assumption is affirmed that there is a causal connection between the investment action and the action of a corresponding object of investment. In our case, this assumption seems plausible for good reasons. If a private investor invests in shares, he becomes a co-owner of a company. The investor provides equity and in return receives the right to dividends as well as privileged access to information concerning the strategy and business conduct. The risk capital provided by the investor is a necessary prerequisite for the management of the object of investment. The greater the participation of a shareholder or the more numerous the number of shareholders, the stronger he, she, or they, can influence a company and provide incentives to behave in a morally consistent manner. A causal connection between the investment activity and its positive influence on the moral conduct of the invested companies can thus be plausibly established in theory. In practice, this causal relationship and the investor's degree of influence can even be promoted and measured by the investor through a conscious selection of investment properties and projects. In such a case, an investor then positively selects his or her investments according to certain investment criteria that are morally eligible. In recent times, this approach of a positive selection and justification of ethical investments, for example in the form of so-called "impact investing", has become increasingly popular in practice.

Nevertheless, the assumption of a general causal relationship between the investment activity and the moral behaviour of companies also has its limits. These are due to information asymmetries and problems of control between shareholders and companies. From a distance, an investor can never comprehensively assess and fully control the actions of his object of investment due to incomplete contracts. In addition, an investor is only one of many factors influencing a company's actions. This argument is therefore likely to weaken the moral justification of investments, solely for objective reasons.

A balancing judgement between moral and financial criteria presupposes not only the causal relationship between investment action and morally assessable action of the target of investment mentioned above. A second important condition for a well-founded judgement is a set of binding moral criteria according to which the actions of companies can be evaluated. It is precisely at this point, however, that the moral justification of investments finds an important practical and theoretical limit.

In practice – and to a large extent in theory too – it is often explicitly assumed that ethical investments should be based on the moral norms and values of *the investor*. It is thus assumed that the investor can and *should* compile his own collection of values and standards. Thus, the moral conduct of companies should be assessed in line with the investor's criteria and ethics funds should be constructed according to his subjective criteria. If one continues this line of thought, then eventually each financial investment could be considered "ethical investing", as long as it is aligned with the individual morals of the investor. Ethical investing then runs the risk of becoming arbitrary, as it is not guided by a binding and universally accepted collection of norms, which is and *should* create the basis of ethical investing.

The question of a collection of moral criteria with a high degree of binding force lies at the centre of the discussion about the opportunities and challenges of morally justified investment. This question can only be addressed meaningfully on the basis of an ethical theory. The theory and method of the FHG, is claimed to represent such a theoretically and methodologically sound approach to deriving moral criteria.

As discussed in Section 3.2, the FHG assumes a universal pluralism of values and bases its justification of moral criteria on a discursive and integrative approach as well as a preference-utilitarian theory and method. A selection of the approximately 850 recommended criteria for assessing the moral conduct of companies are based on fundamental norms and values such as human rights or the moral rules laid out by Gert. It is a fundamental opportunity for ethical investing to be guided by universally valid, binding, and recognised criteria of this kind. The condition to take fundamental norms and values into account when investing would be ethically plausible and justifiable and could be made binding with good reason. It would potentially contribute to a desirable standardisation, comparability, and transparency of the structures and processes of ethical investment.

However, the argumentative potential of such a justification approach for ethical investing is far from being fully tapped in the specific case of the FHG. In the FHG, on the one hand, the collection of criteria clearly appears to be too comprehensive and on the other hand, the FHG deliberately does not express its opinion on the character and degree of commitment of the recommended criteria. Norms and values, the unconditional validity and binding character of which should be justified by reason, as well as claimed – such as the observance of human rights by companies or the avoidance of child labour – are listed in the FHG alongside values such as the desirable renunciation of comparative advertising by a company or the appreciation of a company for remuneration far above the wage agreement. In this context, reasoned and binding rules lose their normative power. This deficiency is exacerbated by the fact that such morally justified criteria, which can and *should* demand a high degree of normative commitment, are also considered possible to be offset by other criteria on the basis of the underlying preference-utilitarian theory. However, as criteria can be selected by a user and can also be compensated for by other criteria, the danger arises of them appearing arbitrary. This is the real weakness of a theoretical approach that justifies a moral collection of criteria on the basis of preference utilitarianism, for which the FHG has been criticised.

The opportunity of a preference-utilitarian (consequentialist-teleological) theory as used by the FHG, however, lies in the fact that its methodology is highly compatible with the economic rationality prevailing in the financial services industry. This factual aspect of the reference to reality of an ethical theory must not be underestimated if applied ethics are to be effective in practice. The FHG's instrumental approach of selecting, weighting, and rating moral criteria has practical strengths, as it is compatible with the justification and selection procedures for stock selection – as practised by investors and players in the financial services industry for conventional investments too. This may be one of several reasons why today, ethical investment funds with huge volumes of assets are guided by a version of the FHG criteria collection, base their "best-in-class" stock selection procedure on these criteria, and align to the FHG methodology.

In order to weigh up the moral and financial criteria of an investment against each other, a systematic ethical investigation must consider two directions at the same time. One concerns the assessment of the moral conduct of companies as objects of investment. This view establishes the basis of the FHG. The second questions the actions of an investor him- or herself as well as the normative status of ethical investing as an investment activity as such. This second issue inevitably arises if one assumes that ethical investing assumes a causal chain between the investment activity and the morally assessable actions of companies.

But are there any good reasons why an investor should be required to fulfil a positive obligation to select his or her investments according to moral criteria? Due to the broad definition of the term "ethical investing" and the situation-specific large differences of investment activities in practice, such a requirement is theoretically hardly justified. Ethical investing can be classified as a special case of an imperfect duty in the Kantian sense, i.e., it is not subject to any demands from those concerned and that the act of investing itself is under-determined.

The term "ethical investing" is too broadly defined to be clearly classified as either a duty to be charitable or as a (strong) positive duty or as a supererogatory act. If one were to define the term very narrowly, at best the (negative) obligation not to invest in companies that violate unconditional moral rights could be defined. In this case, a normative rule would thus be formulated as a duty to negatively select investments, as it is already applied by the historical precursors of ethical investing.

If, however, for pragmatic reasons, the established broad concept of ethical investing is followed, it is difficult to establish a positive obligation to ethical investing. Ethical investing can then be considered a category within the border area between a charitable duty and a supererogatory act, and must be assessed on a case-by-case basis. In any case an assessment here also depends on the underlying ethical theory and the associated narrow or vast character of the underlying concept of duty. The narrower the concept of duty, the more likely it is that a broad concept of ethical investing will go beyond the concept of duty. In this case, ethical investing appears to be a supererogatory act which, although it can be judged as morally good, is not binding.

What do the considerations made so far mean for the fundamental question of how to justify a judgement of balancing between moral and financial criteria? A well-founded collection of criteria for the selection of morally justifiable investments is a necessary condition for ethical investing. Even well-founded moral criteria for investment must ultimately be weighed up against the financial reason of any loss of return for the investor. Therefore the investor himself must carry out further steps of mediation. In the present study, two approaches were proposed which appear promising and interesting for further scientific discussion: Ross's pluralistic deontological approach and the middle-level rules presented by the authors Gabriel/Schlagnitweit.

Ross's approach distinguishes six or seven prima facie duties, "conditional duties", which are to be observed as assessment principles for weighing up conflicting standards against each other in a situation of application. Ross mentions, among other things, the duty of non-maleficence, the duty of justice, the duty of beneficence as well as the duty of self-improvement. The present investigation suggests that these duties should be interpreted in the light of the investment activities of a private investor. They could serve as a possible benchmark against which concrete moral and financial criteria of investment can be measured and weighed up against each other on a meta-level. In particular, the duty of justice, which is defined as the duty to establish distributive justice, could serve here to find further arguments in a balancing judgement.

For further investigation, the middle-level rules recommended by Gabriel/Schlagnitweit could also contribute to clarifying the reason of balancing judgements in areas of normative conflict. On the one hand, these rules are characterised by the fact that they suggest a realistic procedural approach for a private investor in order to be able to independently judge even in opaque moral decision-making situations. Minimizing harm and weighing up goods are the main normative guidelines considered. On the other hand, Gabriel/Schlagnitweit's approach appears to go further in demanding that, in addition to objective aspects, subjective aspects should be included in a balancing judgement too: The ethical investment competence of the investor, which must be trained in an iterative process of learning and development. With regard to this dimension, ethical investing could not only be seen as an action that morally justifies investment actions, but also as a process that requires that moral responsibility be assumed on an individual basis and competence in ethical investing be acquired autonomously.

In its cover story, the weekly magazine Die Zeit asked "*Does money make you immoral?*".[210] Perhaps, one would like to answer, but the chances for morally justified investments are increasing. In its stock market section in August 2013, the Neue Zürcher Zeitung writes.

---

210 Bund/Lebert/Kotynek (2013) 1.

"Not in the least as a result of the financial crisis, many wealthy clients have internalised a new aspect of financial thinking that is no longer focused exclusively on making a profit, but also on generating social added value. … While the connection between morality and economics, i.e., between ethical and economic action, seemed to have disappeared some time ago, the crisis of trust in the financial services sector has shown more impressively than ever that market events cannot be viewed in isolation from the rest of the world and has led to a rediscovery of morality. … Today more than ever, one wants to increase one's wealth with a clear conscience or to effectively give back from what one has. … One would like to engage and not simply leave things to take their course and know that the added value of one's actions is still realised during one's lifetime."[211]

211 Forstinger (2013) 28, translated by the author [MS].

6 The Swiss National Bank's (SNB) investments in equities. A case study

The first version of the present study was completed at the end of 2013. In January 2014, however, public interest in "ethical" investing in Switzerland suddenly grew. The media's attention was triggered by information about the Swiss National Bank's (SNB) morally questionable equity investments, which had suddenly become public as a result of American disclosure requirements. The SNB had invested several million US dollars in cluster bomb production companies.[212] This situation prompted the press to engage in a controversial public debate on the fundamental issues of ethically responsible investment.[213] This controversy in turn triggered the announcement of a turnaround in the SNB's investment policy within just a few days.[214]

The SNB case is instructive. So we shall look at it more closely as a compelling study on ethical investing. The analysis of the SNB's investment decisions and the ethical issues associated with them help elaborate prior considerations and illustrate their practical relevance.

In order to deepen the subject matter, some factual and ethical challenges that institutional investors, such as the SNB, face will be identified in a first step. So far, the present study had primarily placed the investment behaviour of the private investor at the centre of ethical reflection.

---

212 Cf. Bruppacher (2014a) 1; Bruppacher (2014b) 3 and Schmid (2014a) 1; Schmid 2014 (b) 1.

213 Cf. Aiolfi (2014) 27; Enz (2014b) 26; Rasic (2014a) 5; Rasic (2014b) 1; Rasic (2014c) 11; n.s. (2014a) 23; n.s. (2014b) 28.

214 Cf. Schmid (2014b) 1 and Rasic (2014b) 1. Three years after the publication of the first edition of the present study, i.e., in 2017, the topic is still experiencing a certain expansion. In 2017 the largest Swiss pension fund, Publica, refuses titles of selected arms manufacturers and the Verein für verantwortungsbewusste Kapitalanlagen (SVVK) recommends for its members to consider an exclusion list of 15 companies that produce controversial weapons, e.g., General Dynamics, Lockheed Martin, Textron. Cf. Enz (2017) 25 and Schäfer (2017) 24.

In addition, based on some voices from the media, the typical positions for and against ethical investment in public discourse will be presented and classified in the context of this case study.

The purpose of the following remarks is not to join the multitude of accusations that denounce the SNB of ethical misconduct from a distance and seek to scandalise the facts recently uncovered.

6.1 Public moral criticism of SNB investments

At the end of 2013, the SNB invested around 70 billion Swiss francs (CHF) worldwide in equities, of which around 24 billion US dollars were invested in American equities. In the past, these investments were always kept secret and representatives of the national bank did not comment on the targets of their investments.[215]

However, the US Securities Exchange Act requires institutional investors to disclose their equity holdings if they exceed USD 100 million in companies traded at US stock exchanges. As the SNB had crossed that threshold by the end of 2013, the US companies held in the SNB portfolio become publicly known. The US Securities and Exchange Commission (SEC) published the list of these approximately 2,500 companies on the Internet. An analysis of this list shows the following.[216]

The SNB's US equity holdings are broadly diversified. The SNB holds shares in companies from virtually all listed US corporations with the exception of banks, thereby seeking to avoid conflicts of interest with its own monetary policy. The SNB stock portfolio includes, for example, large corporations such as General Electric, oil multinationals such as Exxon Mobil, trading companies such as Wal-Mart, pharmaceutical giants such as Pfizer, beverage companies such as Coca Cola and technology companies such as Apple. Also included are exotic shares such as an investment in the casino company Las Vegas Sands or in the boxing promoter World Wrestling Entertainment.[217]

215 Cf. Bruppacher (2014a) 1; Bruppacher (2014b) 3; n.s. (2014a) 23.
216 Cf. Bruppacher (2014a) 1 and Bruppacher (2014b) 3.
217 Cf. n.s. (2014a) 23; Bruppacher (2014a) 1; Bruppacher (2014b) 3.

The SNB also invests in the five largest armament groups. It owns shares in BOEING (USD 93 million), HONEYWELL INTERNATIONAL (USD 67 million), LOCKHEED MARTIN (USD 38 million), and NORTHROP GRUMMAN (USD 23 million). The latter three are involved in the production of nuclear weapons. In addition, the SNB held co-ownership in the form of shares in GENERAL DYNAMICS (USD 29 million), RAYTHEON (USD 27 million), and TEXTRON (USD 8 million). RAYTHEON has built cluster bombs, GENERAL DYNAMICS and TEXTRON still produce cluster bombs and artillery ammunition.[218]

In particular, the fact that the SNB was investing Swiss national wealth to finance the production of cluster bombs alarmed the public.[219] In the public controversy, economic, legal, and moral arguments for and against such investments were put forward.

The validity and systematic ethical examination of these arguments must first be placed in the context of the SNB's institutionally embedded investment policy. The objective principles of the SNB's investment policy are therefore outlined below in order to provide a more in-depth view of the ethical and legal issues involved.

6.2 Investment policy of the SNB and passive investment in a stock index

The main features of the SNB's investment policy are set out in writing in the "Investment Policy Guidelines of the SNB"[220]. The purpose of these investment guidelines is to clarify the scope of the investment policy. The SNB describes it as follows.

> "These guidelines define the scope of the Swiss National Bank's (SNB) investment activity and make this scope transparent to the public. ... They detail the investments ... which the SNB may execute into in order to perform its investment policy tasks. In particular, the guidelines lay down the investment policy principles, the eligible asset categories and instruments, and the investment and risk control process."[221]

---

218 Cf. Rasic (2014c) 11; n.s. (2014a) 23.
219 Cf. Rasic (2014c) 11; Rasic (2014a) 5; Rasic (2014b) 1.
220 SNB Direktorium (2008).
221 Cf. SNB Governing Board (2008) 1.

The SNB also elaborates on the principles of its investment policy and the permitted investment instruments in its guidelines.[222]

> "When investing assets, the SNB focuses on the criteria of security, liquidity, and return. ... Shares of foreign companies that are part of the relevant share indices of MSCI [MS: Morgan Stanley Capital International] are permitted. These are listed shares with a sufficiently large market capitalisation and liquidity."[223]

According to the SNB guidelines, responsibility for the management of assets is functionally shared among various bodies and persons. The SNB Board of Directors is responsible for defining and annually reviewing the investment strategy, while an internal investment committee is responsible for implementation. As part of the operational process, internal as well as external portfolio managers manage selected investment portfolios. This management is guided by current market indices, which are passively tracked. Risk management professionals continuously monitor the entire investment process.[224]

A passive investment strategy means that in selecting and weighting its investments, the SNB follows the selection and weighting of the shares of a selected equity index as closely as possible. The SNB acquires a broadly mixed basket of shares, the composition of which corresponds to one of many share indices, in this case the common index of the company MSCI (Morgan Stanley Capital International). Unlike an active investor, the SNB, as a passive investor, does not select its equity investments individually. Rather, the SNB copies the composition of the index as accurately as possible in its equity portfolios. Passive investing is therefore also referred to as index investment and is a widespread investment practice. Compared to active investing, passive investing has various advantages, e.g., a high degree of security through broad diversification and an attractive return with low investment costs.[225] Passive investing therefore seems to correspond well to

222 In addition to the equities mentioned in the quotation, the permitted investments also include bonds, gold, currencies and derivatives. See SNB Governing Board (2008) 2 f.

223 SNB Governing Board (2008) 2 f. Translated by the author [MS].

224 Cf. SNB Governing Board (2008) 3 f.

225 On passive investing cf. Bogle (2007); cf. also Goldie/Murray (2011) 45–49.

the SNB's explicitly formulated financial investment objectives of security, liquidity, and return.

The SNB's investment policy guidelines describe the passive investment strategy as follows.

> "The Swiss franc securities and the equity portfolios are managed passively. The equity portfolios track broad market indices. ... Risk management is responsible for the risk analysis, monitoring, and reporting throughout the entire investment process. As part of risk control, compliance with all the requirements of the Board of Directors and all investment guidelines is ensured."[226]

Passive investments by the SNB are made through direct investments in companies and not through funds.[227] However, the basic principle of passive investing is systematically breached in certain exceptional cases. In order to avoid conflicts of interest, for example, the SNB deliberately makes no investments in banks. Investments in shares of Swiss companies are also explicitly excluded in order to avoid unintentional market signals.[228]

The SNB did not appear to apply additional exclusion criteria, e.g., due to ethical considerations, in the selection of its equity investments up until the end of 2013. According to BRUPPACHER, the SNB responded to media inquiries about its ethically controversial investment strategy with the following words.

> "The equity portfolios exclusively serve the long-term optimisation of the risk-return profile of the currency reserves. They are passively managed by tracking a combination of different indices."[229]

According to BRUPPACHER, the SNB deliberately leaves the question open, whether ethical criteria are also considered in stock selection. BRUPPACHER comments critically on this.

> "The national bank would be well advised to include ethical criteria in its strategy in addition to market criteria. And to communicate this in an appropriate way. Otherwise the impression is conveyed that anything goes. Which cannot be a maxim in the administration of national wealth."[230]

226 SNB Governing Board (2008) 4, translated by the author [MS].
227 Cf. n.s. (2014a) 23.
228 Cf. SNB Governing Board (2008) 3.
229 Bruppacher (2014b) 3, translated by the author [MS]; cf. also Schmid (2014a) 2.
230 Bruppacher (2014b) 3, translated by the author [MS].

In the following subchapter, the ethical and legal issues of the SNB's investment policy are examined in greater detail. Before doing so, we would like to draw a brief interim conclusion on some important similarities and differences between the investment behaviour of the institutional investor SNB and the investment behaviour of a private investor.

As an institutional investor, the SNB is obviously initially subject to the same conflict of objectives as a private investor.[231] Financial investment objectives (return, liquidity, and security) on the one hand, and the observance of morally justifiable investment criteria (use of funds by the target of investment) on the other, are potentially in conflict.

Compared to a private investor, however, the SNB has additional objectives and restrictions to consider. The SNB's investment policy is subject to the primacy of monetary and currency policy,[232] and the SNB ultimately does not manage its own assets, but the Swiss national wealth.

In order to achieve its investment objectives, the SNB initially only takes the economic rationale of its investments into account. It sets out the financial goals of return, liquidity, and security in its investment guidelines and strives to achieve these goals as cost-effectively as possible, in this case through a passively implemented investment strategy.

The SNB did not include moral criteria in its written investment guidelines or in its implementation and risk control processes (as of 2014). In any case, a collection of ethical investment criteria was not evident in the investment policy guidelines, with the exception of the explicitly mentioned prevention of conflicts of interest when investing in banks.

In contrast to a private investor, the national bank regularly and systematically invests very large volumes of assets on the capital market with a currency reserve of around CHF 435 billion, of which around CHF 70 billion in equities (information as of 2013).[233] In order to fulfil its mission, it has extensive knowledge, tools, and sources of information on financial issues. It also possesses a professional risk management expertise. The SNB has a huge volume of assets at its disposal, *objectively* as well as

---

231 Cf. Section 2.3 of this study for a detailed discussion of this conflict of objectives.
232 Cf. SNB Governing Board (2008) 1.
233 Cf. n.s. (2014a) 23.

subjectively. Objectively, it controls hundreds of billions of Swiss francs in assets; subjectively, it has, as an institution, far above-average expertise in financial investment.

If we now follow the principle of an investor's moral obligation depending on his capability, as discussed in Chapter 4 of the present study, the investment behaviour of the SNB could require a very high moral benchmark for the selection of investment properties. Due to the available investment volume, the SNB potentially has a large influence on the selected investment properties (e.g., their financing and their share price) and it knows the spectrum of alternative investment opportunities very well.

In spite of its enormous amount of assets and its pronounced financial expertise, the SNB initially appears to have difficulties in recognizing moral issues in its investment behaviour. This thesis is supported in the least by the SNB's direct reactions to media inquiries about its investment behaviour.[234]

In the course of the ongoing public debate about the SNB's reputation, the SNB then revised its initial lack of sensitivity to the issue. It is possible, however, that this adjustment was rather made for strategic reasons and in order to protect their own reputation, than for moral reasons. Irrespective of the SNB's motives for later adapting its investment behaviour, this example impressively illustrates that the growing transparency, identified in Chapter 2 as a significant driving force for the increase in the importance of morally justified forms of investment, is clearly having an impact.

There are probably two main reasons why the SNB initially found it difficult to take ethical criteria into account in its investment process. First, a systemic cause rooted in the division of labour and the passive investment process of the SNB. The danger of a lack of imputability of responsibility and consequently of an institutional diffusion of responsibility arises here. Second, there appears to be a fundamental lack of normative consensus on possible moral criteria, which should be taken into account.

(1) Systemically, the SNB's initially low level of awareness of the issue is probably attributable to a diffusion of responsibility within the organisation. The SNB's investment process is divided into different functions, persons, and hierarchical levels. Compared to the

234 Cf. Schmid (2014a) 2.

investment of a private investor, the formulation of the investment strategy and its implementation is significantly more complex at the SNB, and it is therefore more difficult to clearly assign responsibility to individual actors. The danger may arise that the responsibility for the selection of morally questionable objects of investment cannot be clearly and unambiguously assigned. This danger is not specific to the SNB, but potentially exists in every investment process of an institutional investor that is divided up into parts. This risk is further aggravated by the passive investment strategy pursued, because in this case the SNB in fact delegates the specific selection of investment properties to an index provider.[235]

(2) In addition, there is likely to be a lack of consensus among those responsible at the SNB on the non-economic criteria for responsible investment. The explicit consideration of moral goods does not seem to play an important role vis-à-vis financial objectives (return, liquidity, and security) and was not reflected in the investment guidelines. The moral and legal dimensions of this issue will be analysed in greater depth below.

6.3 Ethical and legal considerations about investing in cluster bombs

The issue of financing cluster bomb producers or banks' shares in cluster munition producing companies is not fundamentally new. Non-governmental organisations (NGOs) such as IKV Pax Christi (Utrecht, NL),[236] FairFin (formerly: Netwerk Vlaanderen, Belgium) or Handicap International (Geneva) have been campaigning transnationally for years to ban cluster bombs, with ever increasing success.[237]

---

235 IKV Pax Christi recommends that the index providers themselves should exclude cluster bomb manufacturers from their share indices. Cf. IKV Pax Christi (2013) 17.

236 Cf. the comprehensive study by IKV Pax Christi (2013). See also n.s. (2010) 2 f to the similar discussion that various NGOs already held with the major Swiss banks UBS and Credit Suisse in 2010. Switzerland signed the UN Convention on Cluster Munitions in 2010, but had not yet ratified it. Cf. also Fischer (2013) 1.

237 Cf. IKV Pax Christi (2013) 8; Rasic (2014c) 11; n.s. (2011) 2.

The process of SNB investment in cluster bomb producers is, however, a prime example, which illustrates the controversial core elements of ethical investing, which were discussed in detail in this study. In the case of the SNB, the following elements of the chain of argumentation can be illustrated in an exemplary way.

(1) *Prohibition of killing, or non-maleficence as a universally binding moral norm.* A clearly defined moral norm with a high degree of universal commitment is up for debate and can guide criteria of ethical investing.[238]
(2) The Swiss Federal Act on War Material (WMA) *assumes a causal connection* between the financing of a cluster bomb company by an investor and the morally and conventionally outlawed actions of this company. In this case, the assumed connection is legally standardised in the form of a law and reinforced with threats of punishment for culpable violations.[239]
(3) In the case of the *indirect financing* of cluster bomb producers as targets of investment, there is nevertheless *a legal and moral grey area* with regard to the question of whether the investor can be held liable in the *absence of intent.*[240]
(4) For a qualified, institutional, and publicly exposed investor such as the SNB, there is a particular *need* in this context to *make a well-founded judgement* on the priority of moral and legal norms and goods on the one hand, and financial objectives on the other. However, the SNB only recognises this need for consideration under public pressure, which is likely to cast doubt on the SNB's moral reputation and power of judgement.

The preceding chain of argumentation will be further explored below.

---

238 For a discussion on the prioritisation and binding nature of moral norms, cf. Section 3.3 in detail.
239 Cf. IKV Pax Christi (2013) 141–143.
240 Cf. IKV Pax Christi (2013) 141–143.

6.3.1 Cluster bombs damage human life and are internationally banned

With the SNB's investment in cluster bomb producers, the identification of the moral good or moral norm in question is relatively simple and undisputed. The core issue is the prohibition of killing humans or the prima facie duty of non-maleficence. This moral good or moral duty is recognised by a high degree of commitment across cultures. This concerns the 'inner core' of morality, which is capable of consensus.[241]

For this reason, an international agreement on cluster munitions, the so-called UN Convention on Cluster Munitions, was brought into force internationally in 2010. This has so far been ratified by 120 states, including Switzerland, and signed by additional 14.[242]

The fact that the financing, production, and use of cluster munitions, which are banned internationally, violate the respect for human life in a particular way can be explained by the way cluster munitions work. Cluster bombs consist of containers with smaller pieces of ammunition. The uncontrolled dispersion of unexploded ammunition poses a long-term threat to the civilian population. This particularly affects children who consider the unexploded ammunition to be toys. The explosion of dud bombs often kills or mutilates innocent children even in times of peace.[243]

6.3.2 Federal Act on War Material prohibits financing cluster bomb production

For this reason, the financing, production and use of cluster munitions is now internationally banned in many countries. Based on the ethical debate that has taken place in recent years, the issue has taken on a legal dimension in addition to the moral dimension in some countries, including Switzerland.[244]

---

241 Cf. the discussion in Chapter 3 of this study and Birnbacher (2013) 83.
242 Cf. IKV Pax Christi (2013) 30; Rasic (2014c) 11; n.s. (2011) 2; www.clusterconvention.org (accessed April 4th, 2019).
243 Cf. Rasic (2014c) 11.
244 Cf. IKV Pax Christi (2013) 141–143; not applicable (2010); n.s. (2011).

Today, cluster bomb producers such as TEXTRON are on the black lists of some international organisations, some (Swiss) commercial banks, certain state funds and private funds that have subjected themselves independently – partly under public pressure – to ethical investment guidelines. Moreover, in its Federal Act on War Material (WMA), which was revised in 2013, Switzerland prohibits the financing of companies that produce cluster bombs and threatens punishment in the event of violation.[245]

Swiss law assumes a causal link between the financing of a company and the company's behaviour, which is morally and conventionally banned. At least in part, however, the legislator in the WMA breaches the principle of the presumption of responsibility and fault of the investor.

6.3.3 Indirect financing is a legal and moral grey area

RASIC points out that there are loopholes in the WMA that the SNB can refer to in its investment behaviour. She writes the following.

> "The fact that investments are still being made in these companies despite the law is partly due to two articles in the Federal Act on War Material.
>
> - For example, if the offender merely accepts the possibility of violating the financing prohibition, she is not liable to prosecution (Article 35b(3) of the WMA). This way, unintentional investments in such companies (e.g., through shares that only constitute a part of a larger financial market product) should not be punished. ...
> - Direct investments in the companies concerned (e.g., lending is mentioned in the law as an example) are explicitly prohibited. Indirect financing (more precisely, holding bonds or other investment products) is prohibited if it is intended to circumvent direct financing (Article 8c(1) and (2) of the WMA)."[246]

This latter definition of indirect financing seeks to protect investors who invest in cluster munitions without direct intent. From a legal point of view, this formulation represents a possible loophole. In practice, the WMA can therefore hardly be brought into action against an investor in a case such as the SNB investment.[247]

---

245 Cf. IKV Pax Christi (2013) 141–143; Rasic (2014c) 11.

246 Rasic (2014c) 11, translated by the author [MS]; cf. IKV Pax Christi (2013) 141–143 for details.

247 Cf. Rasic (2014c) 11.

6.3.4 No moral evaluation of financial goods by the SNB

It would appear that the SNB did not deliberately violate the WMA and is therefore unlikely to be prosecuted. With its one-sided focus on the financial criteria of investment, however, it obviously operates in a legal and moral grey area in this specific case. At the very least, it exposes itself to the suspicion of violating a law or blurring the interpretation.

Irrespective of the legal situation, the SNB appears to interpret the degree of its moral obligation as an influential investor in the financial market very narrowly. Its investment behaviour is remarkable in the sense that a real, significant conflict between moral and financial goals is not recognisable as such. Neither is the controversial investment necessary in order to fulfil the central bank's purpose as the custodian of the currency, nor does the controversial investment seem to contribute in a particular way – or in a better way than any alternative investment opportunity – to the fulfilment of the SNB's financial investment objectives.

Chapter 4 of the present study, based on the authors GABRIEL/SCHLAGNITWEIT, identified four principles, which support the orientation for ethical investing. One of these principles advocates a *"pragmatic, iterative learning process to acquire competence in ethical investing"*. After the press publicly attacked the SNB and cast doubt on its moral reputation, the SNB quickly initiated such a learning process and within days, promised to align its investment criteria with ethical principles.[248] Whether the SNB acted for strategic reasons and to protect its reputation, or out of a moral sense of duty can be left open at this point. According to the statement, the SNB intends to avoid controversial investments going forward and announced in the following media release that, in the future, it intends to follow a selected set of ethical investment criteria.

> "In principle, the Board of Directors has decided to waive shares in companies that produce internationally banned weapons, massively violate fundamental human rights or systematically cause serious environmental damage."[249]

With this statement, the SNB was at least able to calm the media excitement relatively quickly and defuse the public controversy over its investment

---

248 Cf. Schmid (2014a) 1 f.

249 Rasic (2014b) 1, translated by the author [MS]. Cf. also Aiolfi (2014) 27.

policy and moral reputation. How exactly the SNB intends to comply with moral investment criteria shall remain open for the time being and not be further investigated in this study.

6.4 Critique of public moral criticism

In bringing this case study to a close, the focus will be placed on four *positions for and against ethical investing* that appear to be ideal types in the media debate. Each type of argumentation sketched here shall be examined briefly. Each of the following positions has already been discussed in the present study in greater detail: *First:* the primacy of financial goals; *second:* the primacy of legality; *third:* the primacy of laissez-faire; *fourth:* the plea for a morally reflected practice.

This brief synopsis of positions condenses key assumptions that underlie the controversy about "ethical investing". The typology sheds light on the reasons why public opinion cannot yet find a unanimous consent about the moral assessment and the action required in the exemplary situation presented.[250]

6.4.1 The primacy of financial goals

According to this argumentation, financial criteria should take precedence over moral criteria in normative conflicts of investment objectives. In our case study, for example, the argument that the primary institutional purpose of the national bank is to manage the prosperity of the respective country is put forward as a justification.[251]

This task can therefore be achieved in the best possible way by forgoing the consideration of additional investment criteria that could potentially reduce investment returns. Building on this argument, ethical investing is often met with a certain amount of scepticism – sometimes coupled with the argument that a moral justification of investment would overstretch

250 Cf. Rasic (2014a) 1; Aiolfi (2014) 27; Enz (2014a) 35; Enz (2014b) 24; cf. also Feist (2014).

251 Cf. the political comments quoted in Rasic (2014a) 1.

an investor's capability. It would therefore be better to concentrate on achieving a good return on investment or optimising liquidity.[252]

Assessment
This type of argumentation rightly points to the fact that moral criteria of investment are to be assessed in the context of the institutional purpose and within the framework of the normative goals of an organisation. Depending on the purpose and normative requirements of an institution, it seems sensible to set different priorities and weights in conflicts between moral and non-moral norms.

In the specific case of the SNB, however, such an argument is not very persuasive because the primacy of monetary policy obviously does not conflict with the observance of selected moral investment criteria. Neither monetary policy nor the achievement of financial objectives is improved by investing in cluster bomb manufacturers. Only the costs associated with the asset management may be slightly lower when investing in cluster bomb manufacturers as part of a passive investment strategy.[253]

The argument of overstretching moral capacity can be understood. The present study, however, argues that moral responsibility in investment activities should, first, be exercised in accordance with existing competencies and, second, that these subjective competencies should be systematically expanded in a gradual learning process (cf. Section 4.2).

6.4.2 The primacy of legality

This type of argumentation requires that an institutional investor such as the SNB only has to align itself to law and order. If an institution such as the SNB behaves in accordance with the law, it also fulfils its moral obligation. Where the SNB does not explicitly violate laws or conventions, there is therefore no need for action.[254]

---

252 Cf, e.g. Enz (2014a) 35; Enz (2014b) 24 and the quotes in Schmid (2014a) 2 and Rasic (2014a) 5.

253 For the possibility of excluding cluster bomb producers from index investing, see IKV Pax Christi (2013) 17 and the studies mentioned there.

254 A recent article on the investment process of the Compensation Fund (FDC) of the Luxembourg Pension Fund is an example of this argumentation pattern. The FDC already saw itself in the same situation as the SNB in 2010 and has

Assessment
This pattern of argumentation assesses a morally controversial issue exclusively from the aspect of legality. Though this position rightly emphasises that economic actors should align with law and order, in a democratically constituted constitutional state such as Switzerland, this condition is likely to be a necessary but not a sufficient condition for morally responsible conduct. In this pattern of argumentation lies the danger that moral questions coincide with legal questions and that formalistic and legalistic positions are adopted. Though legality and legitimacy (understood here as moral responsibility) can coincide, they do not have to and do not always do so in reality.

In view of our case, this type of argumentation also appears weak because the situation at hand calls for a moral judgement in a legal grey area. Such an interpretation of the law, however, requires a moral deliberation. Law and even legal commentaries can provide assistance for such challenges, but they cannot fully produce an interpretation in a concrete individual case.[255]

6.4.3 The primacy of laissez-faire

This type of argument basically denies the condition of the possibility of a social consensus on binding moral criteria for entrepreneurial action. It is regarded as (too) difficult to define moral criteria of the investment policy and the responsibility for defining such criteria was hardly clearly identifiable in a case such as that of the SNB. For this reason, it would be *best to entirely waive moral investment criteria* and, in this specific case, to continue the SNB's investment policy as before. Elements of this argument are, for example, expressed in a commentary by AIOLFI in the NEUE ZÜRCHER ZEITUNG.

> "Individuals or private companies are free to act according to self-determined ethical rules. In the case of a public institution such as the national bank, however, it is unclear who should be responsible for establishing moral guidelines. There is no binding social consensus on which value systems should apply to

---

since revised its investment process according to ethical investment criteria. However, the term "ethics" is largely interpreted as synonymous with "not legally prohibited." See Feist (2014) 2–3.

255 For the interweaving of moral norms and legal norms see Pieper (2007) 141–143.

companies, and if the SNB intends to act ethically, it must ask itself not only which principles it should observe, but also whose principles. ...

Why should exclusion criteria in an investment policy be limited to weapons, environmental destruction, and human rights violations? Why not include banks with overpaid managers? Or companies with excessively high profits or too low quotas for women? – 'Ethically suspicious' is nothing more than a synonym for 'politically incorrect'. The previous practice of passive index replication may be 'incorrect' in this sense, but it saves the SNB from getting caught up in contradictions."[256]

Assessment

The preceding argumentation sums up the fundamental challenges of an ethically reflected investment, which have been examined in detail in this study. This includes the theoretical difficulty of justifying, prioritising, weighing up, and implementing moral investment criteria in practice (cf. Chapter 3). But not to go down such a path on the grounds that it is demanding and involves contradictions is not a convincing argument. Rather, such an argument seems to fall into the category of those solutions which PAUL WATZLAWICK appropriately refers to as "terrible simplifications"[257]. One refuses to perceive a social reality – in this case an ethically demanding problem – and to address it in a differentiated way because the challenge is very complicated.

This study represents the ideal type of a counter position to the aforementioned type of argumentation. It pleads for an ethically reflected process of investing despite the associated efforts – while being aware of the opportunities and challenges of a moral justification.

6.4.4 The plea for a morally reflected practice

The plea of some voices in the media for a morally reflected investment practice was the trigger for the recent controversy over the SNB's investment practice. In essence, it is about the question of the selection, justification, and weighing up of moral criteria for investment.

Some parties in the media not only take up this question, but at the same time postulate the necessity to identify morally justified investment criteria,

256 Aiolfi (2014) 27, translated by the author [MS].

257 Cf. for this expression Watzlawick/Weakland/Fisch (1984) 60 f.

to communicate them transparently, to implement them consistently, and to further develop them in an evolutionarily manner. Occasionally, other forms of institutionalisation are called for, such as the creation of an ethics advisory board for the SNB.[258]

Assessment
In the controversy described above, only this position appears to be effective. This conclusion is not surprising as this position already represents the framework of the present study.

Of course, in such an ethical discourse the other three positions presented must also be taken seriously. They must be examined at a greater depth for their justifications and ethical background theories and weighed up against each other in the discourse about the better arguments.

Also, a set of instruments – in this case, for example, a collection of moral investment criteria – must neither be developed and applied mechanically nor understood as an end in itself. Moral criteria – and not only those that are to be considered when investing – are to be subjected again and again to the critical judgement of practical reason over the course of time. It is the responsibility of every investor to independently make a normatively justified judgement. This applies to a private investor as well as to an institutional investor such as the SNB. A systematic process of ethical reflection of investment criteria can serve this purpose.

6.4.5 Independent commitment of investors or delegation to third parties?

The present study argues that investors should accept their moral responsibility and should also independently weigh up and decide in moral grey areas. The alternative to the self-determined decision-making process recommended here would be the delegation of moral responsibility to specialised third parties, e.g., financial service providers (banks, asset managers, trustees, associations), supervisory authorities or the regulator.

From the author's point of view [MS], it does not make much sense for the relevant supervisory authorities or the regulator to assume responsibility

258 Cf. also Schmid (2014a) 2; Bruppacher (2014b) 3; Rasic (2014b) 1.

instead of the investor. In practice, it would institutionalise and promote a bureaucratic and legalistic approach. And – more importantly – such an approach is ultimately based on the image of an investor who is unable or unwilling to assume moral responsibility independently.

However, the voluntary delegation of an investor to one or more financial service providers or advisors selected by the investor may be useful. This would be the case if the chosen financial service provider had the appropriate ethical expertise and did not act exclusively in an economic or legalistic manner. In the banking and finance industry, the range of professional services offered in the area of ethical investing is constantly increasing – and investors are increasingly demanding it.

List of figures

Bibliography

Aiolfi, Sergio (2014), Was soll das heissen? ‚Ethisch fragwürdig', in: Neue Zürcher Zeitung, January 23rd, 2014, Nr. 18, p. 27.

Arbeitsgruppe DBK (2010), Mit Geldanlagen die Welt verändern? Eine Orientierungshilfe zum ethikbezogenen Investment, Wissenschaftliche Arbeitsgruppe für weltkirchliche Aufgaben der Deutschen Bischofskonferenz [Ed.], Bonn.

Assländer, Michael/Schenkel, Markus (2009), Vom Guten, vom Schönen und vom Baren: Wie praktikabel ist Ethik als Fondskriterium?, in: Ulshöfer, Gotlind/Bonnet, Gesine [Eds.], Corporate Social Responsibility auf dem Finanzmarkt. Nachhaltiges Investment – politische Strategien – ethische Grundlagen, Wiesbaden, 45–62.

Assländer, Michael/Schumann, Olaf (2011), Wirtschaftsethik als angewandte Ethik, in: Assländer, Michael [Ed.], Handbuch Wirtschaftsethik, Stuttgart, 177–187.

Auerswald, Philip/Quadir, Iqbal [Eds.] (2011), Impact Investing, in: Innovations, Vol. 6, Issue 3, Boston/Massachusetts.

Beck, Andreas/Layes, Gabriel (2017), Ethische Investments aus Sicht der Portfoliotheorie, in: Stüttgen, Manfred [Ed.], Ethik von Banken und Finanzen, Zürich/Baden-Baden, Nomos, 99–115.

Berg, Helmut (2011), Vom Gelde, das dem Leben dient. Mikrofinanz und andere Aspekte sozial verantwortbaren Umgangs mit Geld im Licht der ökonomischen Bedingtheit des Menschen, Frankfurt a.M..

Birnbacher, Dieter (1976), Texte zur Ethik, München.

Birnbacher, Dieter (1995), Tun und Unterlassen, Stuttgart.

Birnbacher, Dieter (2013), Analytische Einführung in die Ethik, Berlin.

Birnbacher, Dieter/Hommen, David (2012), Negative Kausalität, Berlin/Boston.

Bobbert, Monika (2012), Ärztliches Urteilen bei entscheidungsunfähigen Schwerkranken. Geschichte – Theorie – Ethik, Münster.

Bogle, John (2007), The little book of common sense investing: the only way to guarantee your fair share of stock market returns, Hoboken/New Jersey.

Brodbeck, Karl-Heinz (2006), Gewinn und Moral. Beiträge zur Ethik der Finanzmärkte, Aachen.

Bruch, Richard (1981), Die Bevorzugung des kleineren Übels in moraltheologischer Beurteilung. Ein problemgeschichtlicher Durchblick, in: Bruch, Richard, Moralia Varia. Lehrgeschichtliche Untersuchungen zu moraltheologischen Fragen, Düsseldorf, 166–186.

Bruppacher, Balz (2014a), So investiert die Nationalbank, in: Zentralschweiz am Sonntag, January 12th, 2014, Nr. 2, p. 1.

Bruppacher, Balz (2014b), Geheimnis um Aktienanlagen gelüftet, in: Zentralschweiz am Sonntag, January 12th, 2014, Nr. 2, p. 3.

Bund, Kerstin/Lebert, Stephan/Kotynek, Martin (2013), Macht Geld unmoralisch?, in: Die Zeit, Nr. 18, p. 1.

BVV (Versicherungsverein des Bankgewerbes a.G.) (2013), Renteninformation 2013: Informationen zur BVV-Versorgung. Anlage zum Brief an die Rentner und Versicherten, June 2013, Berlin.

Cengiz, Cetin-Behzet/Braun, Dirk/von Nitzsch, Rüdiger (2010), Alpha-Vehikel oder Preis für das gute Gewissen? – Eine Performanceanalyse ethischer Investments, in: Corporate Finance Biz, Issue 4, 263–271.

CRIC (2008), Leitfaden für ethisch orientierte InvestorInnen. Auf was Sie bei einem Beratungsgespräch mit Ihrer Bank achten sollten, CRIC e.V. – Corporate Responsibility Interface Center, Verein für ethisch orientierte Investoren, https://www.cric-online.org/images/individual_upload/cric/cric_leitfaden.pdf, accessed July 21st, 2013.

Cunningham, William (2001), Money and the Spirit, in: Bassler, Karin/Kuhlo, Martinus/Stoll, Peter [Eds.], Ethisches Investment – Strategien für kirchliche Geldanlagen, Stuttgart, 65–78.

Diaz, Michael (2017), Die Sustainable Banking Scorecard. Illustriert am Beispiel der Alternativen Bank Schweiz, in: Stüttgen, Manfred [Ed.] Ethik von Banken und Finanzen, Zürich/Baden-Baden, Nomos, 247–266.

Deml, Max/Blisse, Holger (2011), Grünes Geld. Das Handbuch für ethisch-ökologische Geldanlagen 2012/2013, Stuttgart.

Dierksmeier, Claus (2006), Zur theoretischen Begründung der Wirtschaftsethik, in: Kaatsch, Hans-Jürgen/Rosenau, Hartmut [Eds.], Wirtschaftsethik. Gesammelte Vorträge zur Ringvorlesung Wirtschaftsethik I/II, Münster, 165–189.

Döpfner, Claudia (2000), Zur Glaubwürdigkeit ethisch-ökologischer Geld- und Kapitalanlagen. Eine theologisch-ethische Untersuchung vor dem

Hintergrund der Frage nach der Glaubwürdigkeit der ökonomischen und monetären Strukturen, Frankfurt a.M..

Duchrow, Ulrich (2010), Die Religionen und das Geld, in: Kessler, Wolfgang/Schneeweiss, Antje [Eds.], Geld und Gewissen. Was wir gegen den Crash tun können, Oberursel, 73–96.

EKD (2013), Leitfaden für ethisch nachhaltige Geldanlage in der evangelischen Kirche, 2nd ed., Kirchenamt der Evangelischen Kirche in Deutschland [Eds.], Hannover.

Enz, Werner (2014a), Suva will sozial und ethisch korrekt anlegen, in: Neue Zürcher Zeitung, January 30th, 2014, Nr. 24, p. 35.

Enz, Werner (2014b), Ethisch korrekt investieren. Hehre Absichten und die Gefahr der Überforderung, in: Neue Zürcher Zeitung, January 30th, 2014, Nr. 24, p. 26.

Enz, Werner (2017), Rüstungsaktien auf schwarzer Liste, in: Neue Zürcher Zeitung, March 11th, 2017, p. 25.

Ev. Kirche von Westfalen (2006), Leitfaden zu nachhaltigen Geldanlagen in kirchlichen Haushalten. Materialien für den Dienst in der Evangelischen Kirche von Westfalen, Landeskirchenamt der Evangelischen Kirche von Westfalen [Ed.], Autor: Antje Schneeweiss, Südwind Institute, Bielefeld, https://www.kirchenbund.ch/sites/default/files/media/pdf/themen/kirchliche_pensionskassengelder/Evangelische_Kirche_von_Westfalen_ethische_Geldanlagen.pdf.

Feist, Peter (2014), Die Rentenreserven ethisch verantwortlich investieren. Die guten ins Töpfchen, die schlechten ins Kröpfchen, in: d'Lëtzebuerger Land, January 3rd, 2014, http://www.land.lu/page/article/943/6943/DEU/index.html, accessed June 17th, 2019.

Fischer, Eva Maria (2013), Weltweit Aktionen gegen explosive Investitionen, in: newsroom Handicap International on December 12th, 2013, www.presseportal.de/pm/16206/2620291/weltweit-aktionen-gegen-explosive-investitionen, accessed February 17th, 2014.

FNG (2013), Leitfaden für private Geldanlegerinnen und Anleger: 5 Schritte zur Nachhaltigen Geldanlage, Forum Nachhaltige Geldanlagen, Berlin, http://www.forum-ng.org/images/stories/Publikationen/fng_flyer_anlegerleitfaden.pdf, accessed June 17th, 2019.

Forstinger, Christin (2013), Neue Private Banker braucht das Land. Nötige Berücksichtigung von Philanthropie und Impact Investing, in: Neue Zürcher Zeitung, Nr. 176, p. 28.

Fricke, Anno (2010), Grüne Geldanlage. Verantwortungsvoll investieren, Berlin.

Fünfgeld, Brigitte (2009), Financial Behaviour of Individual Investors in Switzerland: Empirical Evidence, unpublished dissertation from the University of Zürich.

Gabriel, Klaus (2005), Nachhaltigkeitsindizes. Indices of Sustainability, Frankfurt a.M./London.

Gabriel, Klaus (2007), Nachhaltigkeit am Finanzmarkt. Mit ökologisch und sozial verantwortlichen Geldanlagen die Wirtschaft gestalten, München.

Gabriel, Klaus (2008), Ethik in der Geldanlage: Grundlagen, Kriterien und Herausforderungen, in: Faust, Martin/Scholz, Stefan [Eds.], Nachhaltige Geldanlagen – Produkte, Strategien und Beratungskonzepte, Frankfurt a.M., 21–42.

Gabriel, Klaus (2009), Das schnelle Geld. Die Spekulation als solche und ihre ethische Bewertung, in: Hoffmann, Johannes/Scherhorn, Gerhard [Eds.], Eine Politik für Nachhaltigkeit. Neuordnung der Kapital- und Gütermärkte, Erkelenz, 220–236.

Gabriel, Klaus (2012), Auf die Wirkung kommt es an. Ändern nachhaltige Geldanlagen die wirtschaftliche Praxis?, in: Forum Nachhaltig Wirtschaften, Nr. 3, 14–15.

Gabriel, Klaus (2017), Verantwortlich Investierende. Motive, Massstäbe und Handlungsoptionen von Kapitalanlegern, in: Stüttgen, Manfred [Ed.] Ethik von Banken und Finanzen, Zürich/Baden-Baden, Nomos, 57–75.

Gabriel, Klaus/Schlagnitweit, Markus (2009), Das gute Geld. Ethisches Investment, Hintergründe und Möglichkeiten, Innsbruck.

Gert, Bernhard (1983), Die moralischen Regeln. Eine neue rationale Begründung der Moral, Frankfurt a.M..

Goldie, Daniel/Murray, Gordon (2011), The Investment Answer, London.

Graham, Benjamin (2007), Intelligent investieren. Der Bestseller über die richtige Anlagestrategie, München.

Hanke, Karel (1999), Was ist ethisch an „ethischen Geldanlagen"?, in: Bondolfi, Alberto/Münk, Hans [Eds.], Theologische Ethik heute. Antworten für eine humane Zukunft, Zürich, 413–426.

Heinemann, Simone (2017), Finanzderivate und Risikoethik. Zum verantwortungsvollen Umgang mit Risiken auf Finanzmärkten, in: Stüttgen, Manfred [Ed.] Ethik von Banken und Finanzen, Zürich/Baden-Baden, Nomos, 409–429.

Herger, Patrick (2019), Bringen nachhaltige Investments höhere Renditen oder tiefere?, in: Neue Zürcher Zeitung, May 21st, 2019, 19.

Hoffmann, Johannes (2004), Doppelte Dividende: – Ziel der Bewusstseinsbildung für ethische Geldanlagen bei Investoren, Konsumenten und Finanzdienstleistern –, Beitrag zur Festschrift von Franz Josef Stendebach, OMI, zum 70. Geburtstag, Eppenbach, 1–31.

Hoffmann, Johannes/Ott, Konrad/Scherhorn, Gerhard [Eds.] (1997), Der Frankfurt-Hohenheimer Leitfaden, in: Hoffmann, Johannes/Ott, Konrad/Scherhorn, Gerhard [Eds.], Ethische Kriterien für die Bewertung von Unternehmen – Frankfurt Hohenheimer Leitfaden – Deutsch und Englisch, Frankfurt a.M., 1–205.

Hoffmann, Johannes/Scherhorn, Gerhard (2002), Saubere Gewinne. So legen Sie Ihr Geld ethisch-ökologisch an, Freiburg i.Br..

Holderegger, Adrian (1992), Verantwortung, in: Wils, Jean-Pierre/Mieth, Dietmar [Eds.], Grundbegriffe der christlichen Ethik, Paderborn, 199–208.

Horster, Detlef (2009), Ethik, Stuttgart.

Horster, Detlef [Ed.] (2012), Texte zur Ethik, Stuttgart.

IKV Pax Christi (2013), Worldwide Investments in CLUSTER MUNITIONS a Shared Responsibility, Utrecht.

Jahn-Madell, Franziska (2009), Developments on the Ethical Investment Market, in: Hoffmann, Johannes/Scherhorn, Gerhard [Eds.], Eine Politik für Nachhaltigkeit. Neuordnung der Kapital- und Gütermärkte, Erkelenz, 372–396.

Jensen, Michael/Meckling, William (1976), Theory of the firm. Managerial behavior, agency costs, and ownership structure, in: Journal of Financial Economics, Vol. 3, No. 4, 305–360.

Justitia et Pax [Ed.] (1989), Wie verantwortlich Geld anlegen? Anstösse zur Diskussion über kirchliche Geldanlagen, Bern.

Kahnemann, Daniel/Tversky, Amon (1979), Prospect theory: an analysis of decisions under risk, in: Econometrica, Vol. 47, 263–291.

Kersting, Wolfgang (1994), Probleme der Wirtschaftsethik, in: Zeitschrift für philosophische Forschung, Vol. 48, Issue 3, 350–371.

Kersting, Wolfgang (1997), „Das starke Gesetz der Schuldigkeit und das schwächere der Gültigkeit", in: Kersting, Wolfgang [Ed.], Recht, Gerechtigkeit und demokratische Tugend. Abhandlungen zur praktischen Philosophie der Gegenwart, Frankfurt a.M., 74–120.

Klarman, Seth (1991), Margin of Safety: Risk-averse Value Investing Strategies for the Thoughtful Investor, New York.

Kohrs, Thomas/Grün, Anselm (2008), Ethisch Geld anlegen, Münsterschwarzach.

Louche, Céline/Arenas, Daniel/van Cranenburg, Katinka (2012), From Preaching to Investing: Attitudes of Religious Organisations towards Responsible Investment, in: Journal of Business Ethics 110 (3), 301–320.

Lücker, Claus (1999), Zinsverbot und Schuldenerlass – Eine bibeltheologisch-sozialgeschichtliche Studie zur Frage nach ethischen Kriterien für Kapitalanlagen kirchlich-institutioneller Anleger in Deutschland, Frankfurt a.M..

Maniera, Martin (2013), Wachsende Bedeutung von Islamic Finance: die Gebote der Scharia werden nicht immer einheitlich ausgelegt, in: Neue Zürcher Zeitung, Nr. 150, 31.

Mieth, Corinna (2012), Positive Pflichten. Über das Verhältnis von Hilfe und Gerechtigkeit in Bezug auf das Weltarmutsproblem, Berlin.

Missbach, Andreas (2007), Saubere Renditen. Ökologisch und sozial verantwortungsvoll investieren, Bern.

Nell-Breuning, Oswald von (1928), Grundzüge der Börsenmoral: Reprint der Ausgabe von 1928; mit einer Einführung von Friedhelm Hengsbach und Bernhard Emunds (2002), Münster.

Neuhäuser, Christian (2011), Unternehmen als moralische Akteure, Berlin.

n.s. (2010), Schweizer Banken stehen am Pranger wegen Streubomben, in: Tages-Anzeiger, April 15th, 2010, https://www.tagesanzeiger.ch/wirtschaft/unternehmen-und-konjunktur/Schweizer-Banken-stehen-am-Pranger-wegen-Streubomben/story/21608071, accessed June 17th, 2019.

n.s. (2011), Schweizer Banken wegen Streubomben in der Kritik, in: Handelszeitung, May 25th, 2011, www.handelszeitung.ch/unternehmen/schweizer-banken-wegen-streubomben-der-kritik, accessed February 17th, 2014.

n.s. (2013a), Gefragte nachhaltige Anlagen. Deutlicher Zuwachs 2012, in: Neue Zürcher Zeitung, Nr. 109, 28.

n.s. (2013b), Kirchliche Hilfswerke attackieren Kupferkonzern Glencore-Xstrata. Tagebau auf Philippinen könnte Menschenrechte verletzen, in: Neue Zürcher Zeitung, Nr. 133, 13.

n.s. (2014a), Schweizer Nationalbank besitzt Casinos, in: Frankfurter Allgemeine Zeitung, January 14th, 2014, p. 23.

n.s. (2014b), Die zweifelhaften Anlagen der Schweizer Notenbank, in: Handelsblatt, January 15th, 2014, 28.

Oehri, Oliver (2012), Impact – Neues Paradigma für Stiftungen, in: Private Nr. 6, 1.

Ott, Konrad (1997), Erläuterungen zum ethischen Status und zur Methodik des Frankfurt-Hohenheimer Leitfadens, in: Hoffmann, Johannes/Ott, Konrad/Scherhorn, Gerhard [Eds.], Ethische Kriterien für die Bewertung von Unternehmen – Frankfurt Hohenheimer Leitfaden – Deutsch und Englisch, Frankfurt a.M., 207–261.

Pardoe, James (2005), So macht es Warren Buffett. 24 einfache Anlagestrategien des weltweit erfolgreichsten Investors, Wien.

Pennekamp, Johannes (2012), Ethisches Investment: Wie Gutmenschen Geld verdienen, in: Handelsblatt, July 6th, 2012, http://www.handelsblatt.com/politik/oekonomie/nachrichten/ethisches-investment-wie-gutmenschen-geld-verdienen-seite-all/4390044-all.html, accessed July 6th, 2013.

Pieper, Annemarie (2007), Einführung in die Ethik, Tübingen/Basel.

Pinner, Wolgang (2003), Ethische Investments. Rendite mit „sauberen" Fonds, Wiesbaden.

Rasic, Sasa (2014a), Wirbel um Anlagestrategie der Nationalbank, in: Neue Luzerner Zeitung, January 15th, 2014, Nr. 11, p. 5.

Rasic, Sasa (2014b), Die Nationalbank kriegt kalte Füsse, in: Neue Luzerner Zeitung, January 18th, 2014, Nr. 14, p. 1.

Rasic, Sasa (2014c), Volksvermögen für Streubomben, in: Neue Luzerner Zeitung, January 18th, 2014, Nr. 14, p. 11.

Reinhardt, Volker (2009), Mein Geld! Meine Seele! Die grössten Geizhälse und ihre Geschichten, Nördlingen.

Ricken, Friedo (2003), Allgemeine Ethik, 1983, cited from the revised, fourth edition, Stuttgart.

Rockefeller Foundation [Ed.] (2012), Accelerating Impact. Achievements, Challenges and What's Next in Building the Impact Investing Industry, https://www.rockefellerfoundation.org/report/accelerating-impact-achievements/, accessed June 17th, 2019.

Ross, David (1930), The Right and the Good, Oxford.

Ross, David (1976), Ein Katalog von Prima-facie Pflichten (Original: „The Right and the Good" [1930]), in: Birnbacher, Dieter/Hoerster, Norbert [Eds.], Texte zur Ethik, München, 253–269.

Rotthaus, Stephan (2009), Erfolgreich investieren in grüne Geldanlagen. Ökologisch – ethisch – nachhaltig, Frankfurt a.M..

Schäfer, Henry (2001a), Triple Bottom Line Investing – Ethik, Rendite und Risiko in der Kapitalanlage, in: Zeitschrift für das gesamte Kreditwesen, 54, 13, 740–744.

Schäfer, Henry (2001b), Ethisch motiviertes Anlageverhalten deutscher Nonprofit Organisationen mit religiöser Zwecksetzung. Ergebnisse einer explorativen empirischen Erhebung, in: Bassler, Karin/Kuhlo, Martinus/Stoll, Peter [Eds.], Ethisches Investment – Strategien für kirchliche Geldanlagen, Stuttgart, 96–114.

Schäfer, Henry (2011), Ethik und Kapitalmarkt, in: Assländer, Michael [Eds.], Handbuch Wirtschaftsethik, Stuttgart, 366–376.

Schäfer, Michael (2012), Impact-Investing. In eine bessere Welt investieren, in: Neue Zürcher Zeitung, September 20th, 2012, 24.

Schäfer, Michael (2017), Pensionskasse des Bundes stösst Rüstungstitel ab, in: Neue Zürcher Zeitung, June 14th, 2017, p. 24.

Schaefers, Kevin (2013), Nachhaltiges Investieren – ein wirtschaftsethisches Beratungskonzept, Bamberg.

Schaefers, Kevin (2017), Anlageberater und Anlageberatung. Eine investmentethische Untersuchung, in: Stüttgen, Manfred [Ed.] Ethik von Banken und Finanzen, Zürich/Baden-Baden, Nomos, 205–232.

Scherhorn, Gerhard (2008), Ein Plädoyer für die Berücksichtigung ethischer Aspekte bei der Geldanlage, in: Orientierungen zur Wirtschafts- und Gesellschaftspolitik, 118, Nr. 4, 40–46.

Scherhorn, Gerhard (2009a), Die einseitige Verpflichtung der Kapitalgesellschaften auf das Kapitalinteresse, in: Hoffmann, Johannes/Scherhorn, Gerhard [Eds.], Eine Politik für Nachhaltigkeit. Neuordnung der Kapital- und Gütermärkte, 239–256, Erkelenz.

Scherhorn, Gerhard (2009b), Geld soll dienen, nicht herrschen. Die aufhaltsame Expansion des Finanzkapitals, Wien.

Scherhorn, Gerhard (2010), Die soziale Verantwortung des Kapitals. Finanzmärkte und das Nachhaltigkeitsprinzip, in: evangelische Aspekte, Nr. 1, 4–9.

Schneeweiss, Antje (1997), Erfahrungen mit der Überprüfung der Sozialverträglichkeit von Unternehmen, in: Hoffmann, Johannes/Ott, Konrad/Scherhorn, Gerhard [Eds.], Ethische Kriterien für die Bewertung von Unternehmen – Frankfurt Hohenheimer Leitfaden – Deutsch und Englisch, Frankfurt a.M., 333–345.

Schneeweiss, Antje (1998), Mein Geld soll Leben fördern. Hintergrund und Praxis ethischer Geldanlagen, Mainz.

Schneeweiss, Antje (2002), Kursbuch Ethische Geldanlage. Aktien, Fonds, Beteiligungen, (Überarbeitete Neuausgabe von Schneeweiss [1998]), Mainz.

Schneeweiss, Antje (2009), Entwicklungspolitische Kriterien im ethischen Investment. Geldanlagen entwicklungspolitisch und nachhaltig wirksam machen, in: Profil 09, 1–30.

Schneeweiss, Antje (2017), Der Einfluss nachhaltiger Investoren auf Unternehmen. Eine explorative Recherche, in: Stüttgen, Manfred [Ed.] Ethik von Banken und Finanzen, Zürich/Baden-Baden, Nomos, 165–190.

Schmid, Simon (2014a), 690 Millionen Dollar an kritischen Finanzanlagen, in: Tagesanzeiger, January 13th, 2014, http://www.tagesanzeiger.ch/wirtschaft/konjunktur/690-Millionen-Dollar-an-kritischen-Finanzanlagen/story/31842529, accessed February 17th, 2014.

Schmid, Simon (2014b), SNB wirft den Kriegsballast ab, http://www.tagesanzeiger.ch/wirtschaft/unternehmen-und-konjunktur/SNB-wirft-den-Kriegsballast-ab/story/21330343, accessed February 17th, 2014.

Scholand, Markus (2004), Triple Bottom Line Investing und Behavioral Finance. Investorenverhalten als Determinante der Entwicklung nachhaltiger Anlageprodukte, Frankfurt a.M..

Schröder, Michael (2008), Performance nachhaltiger Geldanlagen, in: Faust, Martin/Scholz, Stefan [Eds.], Nachhaltige Geldanlagen – Produkte, Strategien und Beratungskonzepte, Frankfurt a.M., 519–538.

Schwanfelder, Werner (2012), Wie Sie Profit machen und nebenbei die Welt verbessern. Gewinnbringend und nachhaltig investieren, München.

Seiler Zimmermann, Yvonne et al. (2017), Zur Ethik der Terminspekulation auf Rohstoffmärkten, in: Stüttgen, Manfred [Ed.] Ethik von Banken und Finanzen, Zürich/Baden-Baden, Nomos, 431–463.

SNB Direktorium (2008), Richtlinien der Schweizerischen Nationalbank (SNB) für die Anlagepolitik vom 27. Mai 2004 (Stand am 1. April 2015), https://www.snb.ch/de/mmr/reference/snb_legal_richtlinien/source/snb_legal_richtlinien.de.pdf, accessed June 17th, 2019.

Sparkes, Russel (2001), Ethical Investment for the Methodist Church, UK – The Central Finance Board Experience, in: Bassler, Karin/Kuhlo, Martinus/Stoll, Peter [Eds.], Ethisches Investment – Strategien für kirchliche Geldanlagen, Stuttgart, 79–87.

Streiff, Stefan (2017), Ethik-Komitee in der Vermögensverwaltung. Eine deliberative Methode zur Wahrnehmung von Verantwortung im Investmentprozess, in: Stüttgen, Manfred [Ed.] Ethik von Banken und Finanzen, Zürich/Baden-Baden, Nomos, 233–245.

Stüttgen, Manfred (2019a), Mikrokredite. Nachhaltige Geldanlage im Spannungsfeld von Marketing und Moral, in: Stüttgen, Manfred [Ed.] Ethik von Banken und Finanzen, zweite Auflage, Zürich/Baden-Baden, Nomos, 117–139.

Stüttgen, Manfred (2019b), Ethik der Banken? Herausforderungen und Perspektiven, in: Stüttgen, Manfred [Ed.] Ethik von Banken und Finanzen, zweite Auflage, Zürich/Baden-Baden, Nomos, 15–42.

Stüttgen, Manfred/Mattmann, Brian (2017), IFZ Sustainable Investments Studie 2017. Nachhaltige Investmentfonds im Schweizer Vertrieb, Zug.

Stüttgen, Manfred/Mattmann, Brian (2018), IFZ Sustainable Investments Studie 2018. Differenzierung nachhaltiger Anlagen bei Investoren, Zug.

Thurnherr, Urs (2001), Vernetzte Ethik. Zur Moral und Ethik von Lebensformen, Freiburg/München.

Thurnherr, Urs (2010), Angewandte Ethik. Zur Einführung, Hamburg.

Ulrich, Peter/Jäger, Urs/Waxenberger, Bernhard (1998), Prinzipiengeleitetes Investment I. Kritische Analyse der gegenwärtigen Praxis bei „ethisch-ökologischen" Geldanlagen, Institut für Wirtschaftsethik, Beiträge und Berichte Nr. 83, St. Gallen.

Ulshöfer, Gotlind (2008), Corporate Social Responsibility auf den Finanzmärkten: Ebenen der Verantwortung, in: Faust, Martin/Scholz, Stefan [Eds.], Nachhaltige Geldanlagen – Produkte, Strategien und Beratungskonzepte, Frankfurt a.M., 26–44.

Urmson, James (1953), The interpretation of the Moral Philosophy of J.S. Mill, in: The Philosophical Quarterly, 3/10 (1953–01), 33–39.

Urmson, James (1958), Saints and Heroes, in: Melden, A.I. [Ed.], Essays in Moral Philosophy, Seattle, 198–216.

Urmson, James (2003), Eine revidierte Mill-Interpretation, in: Horster, Detlef [Ed.] (2012), Texte zur Ethik, Stuttgart, 258–262.

Urmson, James (2012), Heilige und Helden, übersetzt von Martin-Christoph Just, (Original: „Saints and Heroes" [1958]), in: Horster, Detlef [Ed.], Texte zur Ethik, Stuttgart, 361–384.

Watzlawick, Paul/Weakland, John/Fisch, Richard (1984), Lösungen. Zur Theorie und Praxis menschlichen Wandels, Bern.

Weber, Olaf (2017), Soziale Banken. Chancen und Herausforderungen aus ethischer und ökonomischer Sicht, in: Stüttgen, Manfred [Ed.] Ethik von Banken und Finanzen, Zürich/Baden-Baden, Nomos, 267–289.

Werner, Micha (2011a), Einführung in die philosophische Ethik I: Gegenstand und Aufgabe der Ethik, Fernlehrgang Berater/in für Ethik im Gesundheitswesen, Klinikum Nürnberg, Centrum für Kommunikation Information Bildung, Nürnberg, https://www.micha-h-werner.de/modul01.pdf.

Werner, Micha (2011b), Einführung in die philosophische Ethik II: Methoden und Theorien der Ethik, Fernlehrgang Berater/in für Ethik im Gesundheitswesen, Klinikum Nürnberg, Centrum für Kommunikation Information Bildung, Nürnberg, https://www.micha-h-werner.de/modul02.pdf.

Werner, Micha (2011c), Artikel „Verantwortung", in: Düwell, Marcus/Hübenthal, Christoph/Werner, Micha [Eds.], Handbuch Ethik, 541–548.

Wolbert, Werner (1990), Artikel „Übel", in: Rotter, Hans/Virt, Günter [Eds.], Neues Lexikon der Christlichen Moral, Innsbruck, 806–808.

ZDK (2007), Ethisches Investment – Mit Geldanlagen Verantwortung wahrnehmen! Handreichung für private und kirchliche Anleger, Zentralkomitee der deutschen Katholiken, http://www.zdk.de/veroeffentlichungen/erklaerungen/detail/Ethisches-Investment-Mit-Geldanlagen-Verantwortung-wahrnehmen—162T/, accessed July 6th, 2013.

Index

Index of names

Moderne – Kulturen – Relationen

Herausgegeben von Gerhard Droesser und Ruth Hutzel

Band 1 Gerhard Droesser / Stephan Schirm (Hrsg.): Ethisch moderieren. Bestimmungen demokratischer Lebensformen. 2002.

Band 2 Andreas Heeg: Ethische Verantwortung in der globalisierten Ökonomie. Kritische Rekonstruktion der Unternehmensethikansätze von Horst Steinmann, Peter Ulrich, Karl Homann und Josef Wieland. 2002.

Band 3 Esther Hornung: Bibelpolitik. Das Verhältnis des protestantischen Fundamentalismus zur nationalen Innenpolitik der USA von 1980 bis 1996. Ein Fallbeispiel. 2002.

Band 4 Roy Lazar Anthonisamy: Youth Violence and Pastoral Care. Pastoral Response of the Christian Community towards the Youth who take up Violence for Justice in Post-Colonial India. 2003.

Band 5 Michael Bauer: Entwicklungszusammenarbeit und Breitensport. Theoretische Überlegungen zum Breitensport in der Entwicklungszusammenarbeit und Evaluierung von Breitensportveranstaltungen in Entwicklungs-, Schwellen- und Transformationsländern innerhalb der Förderstrategie des Internationalen Olympischen Komitees. 2004.

Band 6 Gerhard Droesser / Stephan Schirm (Hrsg.): Kreuzungen. Ethische Probleme der modernen Stadt. 2005.

Band 7 Germán Vargas Callejas: Educación y desarrollo en los Andes. Estudio etnográfico de la comunidad Quechua de Aramasí en Bolivia. 2005.

Band 8 Yves Soudan: Rapport aux choses, rapport aux autres. Propriété privée et lien social. 2007.

Band 9 Stephan Wirz: Erfolg und Moral in der Unternehmensführung. Eine ethische Orientierungshilfe im Umgang mit Managementtrends. 2007.

Band 10 Gerhard Droesser / Ralf Lutz / Jochen Sautermeister (Hrsg.): Konkrete Identität. Vergewisserungen des individuellen Selbst. 2009.

Band 11 Raoul Kiyangi Meya: Délinquance et violence juvenile. Pour une éthique de responsabilité en République Démocratique du Congo. 2011.

Band 12 Joachim Riedmayer: Sozialethische Gesichtspunkte der Ökonomisierung des Krankenhauswesens in Deutschland. 2011.

Band 13 Stefan Schenk: Gesellschaft, Sport und Diakonie. Eine sozialethische Studie. 2011.

Band 14 Dorothea Buehler: "There's a Way to Alter the Pain". Biblical Revision and African Tradition in the Fictional Cosmology of Gloria Naylor's *Mama Day* and *Bailey's Café*. 2012.

Band 15 Lebensfragen. Festschrift für Gerfried W. Hunold. Herausgegeben von Gerhard Droesser und Michael Hartlieb. 2013.

Band 16 Sascha Zinn: Bildungsziel Nachhaltigkeit!? Eine interdisziplinäre Reflexion. 2013.

Band 17 Manfred Stüttgen: Ethisch investieren. Chancen und Grenzen moralisch begründeter Geldanlage. 2., überarbeitete Auflage . 2017.

Band 18 Patricia Kemmer: Das Museum als Kompensation? Eine Ausstellungsanalyse des Bachhauses in Eisenach. 2015.

Band 19 Francine Charoy: Vers une éthique de la liberté. Reconstruction de la *conduite de vie* dans la théologie éthique de Trutz Rendtorff. 2015.

Band 20 Mardoeke Boekraad: Ecological Sustainability in Traditional Sámi Beliefs and Rituals. 2016.

Band 21 José Luis Fernández Cadavid: Justicia social y leyes canónicas en Indias. Una provocadora cooperación al desarrollo jurídico-cultural. 2017.

Band 22 Manfred Stüttgen: Ethical Investing. Opportunities and Challenges of Morally Justified Investments. 2019.

www.peterlang.com

www.ingramcontent.com/pod-product-compliance
Ingram Content Group UK Ltd.
Pitfield, Milton Keynes, MK11 3LW, UK
UKHW041829100926
8556IPUK00002B/91

9 783631 789056